THE JOURNEY BEGINS WITH 1,000 MILES

THRIVING WITH PARKINSON'S DISEASE THROUGH HOPE, OPTIMISM, AND PERSEVERANCE

JOHN C. ALEXANDER

Positively Powered

Positively Powered
PO Box 270098
Louisville, CO 80027
UnleashYourInnerAuthor.com

Cover photo by Melissa Lyttle Photography, Los Angeles, CA

Special thanks to The Parkinson's Project (who sponsored that photo shoot) theparkinsonproject.com

Photographs: Courtesy of John Alexander unless otherwise noted

Cover Design: Melody Christian of FinickyDesigns.com

Ordering Information: JohnAlexanderTalks.com

Quantity sales: Special discounts are available on quantity purchases by nonprofit organizations, corporations, associations, and others. For details, contact us at JohnAlexanderTalks.com

The Journey Begins with 1,000 Miles / John C. Alexander —1st ed.

ISBN 978-0-9961692-3-3

Testimonials

For Father's Day, 2017, my daughter-in-law, Jessica, gave me a keychain with the phrase "Pedal On" attached to it, as a reminder of my motto, "Keep Calm, Hug Often, and Pedal On." The company that she ordered it through used her statement below as part of its e-marketing campaign for Father's Day. Such kind words from a lovely lady:

"He has Parkinson's Disease. Through biking, he's found a way to manage the symptoms and live a healthy lifestyle. He's an exceptional father, grandfather, husband, and an example of how all men should live life."
—Jessica Kirby Alexander, Daughter-in-law and half of the Kirby Howell writing team, authors of three young adult books - the *Autumn Series*, including *Autumn in the City of Angels*.

"John's approach to his Parkinson's disease is inspirational. I have marveled at his positive attitude, commitment to exercise, and embrace of new technologies. His eagerness to share his efforts and experiments with other PD patients has helped scores of people deal proactively with the disease. His book will enlighten countless others to improve their outlook and their lives."
—Rita Bornstein, Ph.D., President Emerita , Rollins College, Winter Park, Florida

"John's tremor is on his left side, while mine is on my right. We joke that we can give each other a back massage when we stand next to each other for photos. Today, with his newly fitted DBS, I may have lost my free massage. Don't worry John, I've still got your back! Maintaining a sense of humor and positive outlook are keys to outrunning Parkinson's. It's my pleasure to share the PD journey with people like John."
~Jimmy Choi, PD Hero, Team Fox VIP, American Ninja Warrior

"I've had the privilege of working side-by-side with John Alexander on many industry and volunteer events, I've traveled with him, stayed in his family home and served on not-for-profit boards with him. When my dear father-in-law, Dan Gray, was losing his battle with Parkinson's disease, John supported our family by dedicating to ride 500 miles on his bicycle in Dan's honor. Amazing, Generous, Vibrant, and Encouraging are just a few of the superlatives I've heard others say about my friend John Alexander. Here are some of mine:
Passionate and Positive
Authentic
Respectful
Kilt, yes he wears kilts, as a tribute to his Scottish Heritage!
Involved in worthwhile programs
Nice...one of the Nicest people on the planet.
Servant Leader
Overcoming Obstacles
NOT GONNA GIVE UP, EVER!
Supportive"
    —**Mike Amos**, Past President and Lifetime Member CHART
        (Council of Hotel and Restaurant Trainers)

"I remember John's "first mile" and then later on accompanying him on his epic ascent and descent of Ben A'an. Through John's friendship, openness and motivation, we have maintained our 'Bond across the Pond.'"
    —**Roger H. Barr**, Munro Compleatist and Long-Distance
        Walker, Airdrie, Scotland

"I have a great appreciation for the value of responsibility and one of my favorite quotes is by George L. Bell. 'You can pretend to care but you cannot pretend to show up.' John Alexander is someone who shows up. He is relentless in his shared knowledge and participation in the Parkinson's community, but just as impressive is his authentic support for others. He is a benchmark for my journey through life."
    —**Mark Egeland**, General Manager/Partner of Catrike

"1.5 million people in the US have PD and most, myself included, are like John. We're normal people. We're middle-aged, a little on the heavy side, we have family that needs us and we're just trying our best to push the limits that this stupid disease has put on us. What makes John's experience so special is that John is not a superhero. He's not climbing Mt. Kilimanjaro. He doesn't run marathons. He's not on Dancing with the Stars. His way of living with Parkinson's disease is something anyone can do – if they are motivated to do it. And that's what his story does – it motivates you to step a little outside your comfort zone and to live fully with PD. What John does is live. He smiles. He travels. He talks to people about the challenges. And he never gives up or gives in. Too many books are about people with Parkinson's who do things I wouldn't do even if I didn't have Parkinson's. Here is a book about someone doing what anyone could – and should – do; live, love and laugh through the good times and the bad."

—**Jill Ater**, Person with Parkinson's,
Davis Phinney Foundation Ambassador

"John is an extremely kind, thoughtful and caring man, whom I first met in 2012. He's been a tremendous influence on and inspiration for the Parkinson's community, and he has been a fantastic ambassador for the Davis Phinney Foundation. John is a connector in the community; putting people together and helping magic happen. John started this journey by cycling a thousand miles a year in his quest to live well with Parkinson's and continues to live this message each day."

—**Polly Dawkins**, Executive Director,
Davis Phinney Foundation

"John Alexander approaches life with Parkinson's with a can-do attitude. "What can I do" rather than what can't I do. He inspires those around him with a zest for life and never-give-up attitude. I'm a proud to call John a friend and fellow Parkinson's warrior."

—**Cidney Pratt Donahoo**,
Davis Phinney Foundation Ambassador

"John Alexander is a hero to me in a very personal way. My grandfather, who was the love of my life, had Parkinson's. When I shared his story with John, he organized a Grandparents Ride fundraiser and dedicated 500 miles in honor of my grandpa. In my grandfather's final days I shared with him a video of John speaking when he talked about the ride and my grandfather. My grandfather, who was very weak and ill at the time was so touched, he smiled and teared up. I'll never forget that or how much John's advocacy helped educate and inspire me, and how his big heart made my grandfather feel comfort, love and support. We all hope to move, touch and change lives like John does."
—**Amanda Hite**, Co-Founder and
CEO of Be the Change Revolutions

"In the 20 years that I have known John Alexander, he has always been one of the great ambassadors of the restaurant industry. And yet, that's not the main reason I consider him a rock star. Although John daily and courageously takes on Parkinson's, he has 'outfoxed' the disease with his infectious positivity…and inspired all of us who witnessed him cycle over 3,500 miles and complete two triathlons. The guy is amazing and I am proud to consider him a dear friend. I defy anyone to read The Journey Begins with 1,000 Miles and not be inspired."
—**Jim Knight**, Keynote Speaker and Author, *Culture That Rocks*

"John Alexander is one of those very few people you meet in your lifetime who simply lives an extraordinary life. But there is nothing simple about John! He has successfully turned the diagnosis of Parkinson's disease on its ear by cycling 3,500 miles, climbing a mountain in Scotland, and completing two triathlons. His ordinary, yet extraordinary, story inspires us all to live our lives to the fullest each and every day."
—**Lisa Marovec**, Senior Director of Marketing, CHART — Council of Hotel and Restaurant Trainers

"One symptom that affects some people with Parkinson's is known as "facial masking," in which you have little to no expression and you look dead inside. This is one symptom of PD which John Alexander has never experienced since he is 'Lit Within.' While some people struggle with their shake, John continues to live in spite of it. It is people like John I look up to and smile, because through him I've learned life goes on!"

—**Allie Topperwein**, Nonprofit Founder,
American Ninja Warrior and Parkinson's Disease Fighter

"John Alexander is one of the most energetic, inspiring, positive, and persevering human beings you'll ever find. His journey with Parkinson's has not been an easy one, but his courageous determination and optimistic attitude towards life have given him a tremendous hope that anything you want to achieve in life is possible."

—**Ricardo Villarreal**, Co-Director of the film Ride with Larry

Dedication

This book is dedicated to my wife, Laura. When we exchanged our wedding vows 42 years ago, one of the lines was "for better or worse." One would think that a diagnosis of a progressive, degenerative neurological disease called Parkinson's would surely fall into the worse category, if not THE worst. However, over the past seven years, Laura's support and encouragement of me have actually helped make these some of our best years, during which time our love for each other has grown even stronger. She has been patient when I've had challenges and generous in allowing me to pursue the activities that I need to do to stay as healthy as possible. She gave me the time to participate in my advocacy roles and build my inspirational team of PD Heroes. In return, I have tried to continue to be the cheery person that she married, and will always strive to remain happy and healthy.

In addition, this book is also dedicated to my son, Brian, and daughter, Jennifer. While my diagnosis no doubt came as a shock to them, they have each stood by my side during my cycling and triathlon adventures, and were there for me at the time of my DBS surgery. I am so proud of the wonderful adults they have each become, the terrific spouses that they have chosen in Brian's Jessica and Jen's Bob, and the beautiful grandchildren that they have added to our family.

Lastly, I want to recognize our three grandchildren — Lilly, Lex, and Danny. May you each fulfill your dreams, lead lives of joy and gratitude, and choose to Thrive when times get tough. Grampy may be a "robot" now — running on batteries, but he does so to have more time to spend with each of you.

Love to all my family, *John*

Laura Alexander

The whole family at Universal Studios, CA

Brian and Jessica Alexander

Daniel John Alexander

Jen and Bob Everland

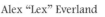

Alex "Lex" Everland

Lillian "Lilly" Everland

Contents

Life is Tough

A DOCTOR ENTERED THE MATERNITY WARD and observed the new mother quietly praying her rosary. Only one baby had been born that day, so it was obviously hers. The baby was premature and it had been touch and go ever since his birth. Dismissing conventional sensitivity altogether, the doctor addressed the woman, "If you are praying for that baby, you would be better praying that he dies. He'll never be normal."

The mother, Josephine Gibson Alexander, simply turned away and continued with her prayers. That doctor had no idea who he was dealing with. A little over a year before, she had lost her third child, Steven, within days of his birth due to an Rh factor incompatibility in his blood. Choosing to have another child had been a risk for both the mother and her fourth offspring. Despite the odds, my mother was bound and determined to get me through this the one way that she knew — with a direct appeal to the Almighty. Many people faced with the need to seek the intervention of a higher power would be asking how to start. For Mom, it was a local call.

1

Her appeal did not fall on deaf ears. I survived the first day, the first week, the first month, and on. It took what I refer to as a "complete oil change," a total of seventeen blood transfusions to pull me through. Those were the selfless gift of my godmother, Harriett Ludwa, a friend of my parents. Right from the start I learned that you get by "with a little help from your friends."

For the first five years, I was quite thin and frequently ill. My mother considered it a positive sign when I started wearing husky sizes in grade school. The predictions of the "good doctor" that I may have suffered brain damage from being deprived of oxygen during my premature birth were unfounded. The only residual effect was a slight vision problem, so I began wearing glasses at age two. My parents entrusted the improvement of my sight to a well-respected local ophthalmologist, Dr. Graham. He worked diligently for several years to improve my vision and had me out of glasses by my senior year in high school. By every account, I had beaten the odds.

Life, as they say, went on. Other than losing my father to a heart attack when I was only 15, I've lived a charmed life. I learned to swim, ride a bike, play baseball, broke a few bones and had my share of scrapes and bruises along the way. I learned to play two musical instruments, made friends, got average grades, graduated from college and graduate school, and have had successful careers. I graduated from The School of Hospitality Business at Michigan State University and managed in hotels and restaurants for about ten years (Beverage Manager for the Hotel St.

Francis and General Manager of a 300-seat casual dining restaurant in San Francisco). I went into sales after that, working for The Quaker Oats Company for about fifteen years, and most recently handled national account sales for the National Restaurant Association. I went back to school (Webster University) and earned my M.A. in Human Resources Development with a focus on training in 2005.

I was fortunate to meet Laura, a wonderful and loving woman, and as of this writing we've sailed through over 42 years of married life. We were blessed with two fantastic children, Brian and Jennifer, and have been privileged to see them grow to be amazing young people. They each found supportive spouses — Brian's Jessica and Jen's Bob. The icing on the cake was Jen giving birth of to our first grandchild, Lilly (July, 2011), followed by her second, Alexander (Lex) (August, 2014). Then Brian's son, Daniel John, was born in January, 2015 to round out the set to three healthy and beautiful grandchildren.

Yes, life has been good.

Perhaps that doctor was right, I never have been just normal. With the love of my parents, brother, sister, aunts, uncles, cousins, friends, and later my wife and our children and grandchildren, I grew to be a joyful person, perhaps average in many ways, maybe even awesome in others — but never just "normal." Life to me has been all about enjoying the ride — constantly learning and growing, helping people connect, and finding the bright side to just about any situation. Not everything has been perfect — after all, the reality is that life is tough. Everyone is hit with the unexpected from time to time. I simply developed a coping mechanism from those very first hours to deal with the bumps along the way.

CHAPTER 1

The Diagnosis

MY MEDICAL HISTORY BY AGE 58 consisted of a tonsillectomy at age nine and eye muscle surgery to correct a lazy eye when I was 45. My fitness and activity level, however, had me on the

Laura and John Alexander

road to some problems. My weight had shot up to 290, and other than huffing and puffing through airports to catch planes, my workout regimen was nonexistent. My blood sugar level put me in the pre-diabetes category. My biggest fear had always been my heart, which was ticking along just fine, though my cardiologist hounded me to lose weight. My father died of a heart attack when he was just 48. I had been anxious when I hit that chrono-

logical milestone. I had already been given ten more years on this earth than my father. It's best to say that I'd been lucky, rather than good.

In September of 2009, Laura and I were headed out to California for a vacation. We would be visiting her sister in the San Francisco Bay Area and attending the Caledonian Club of San Francisco Highlands Games. I became interested in my Scottish heritage about five years earlier and was serving the Clan Macalister Society as its District Commissioner for Florida and Georgia. The group's annual general meeting was being held at this event and I would be stepping into the role of President.

Our bags were packed and I was loading them into the car. A limo driver had once cautioned me to use both the side and top handles when lifting a heavy bag, so I did just that as I placed Laura's suitcase into the trunk. That left just my rolling duffel bag to load. I'd left it standing upright, so I grabbed the strap at the end and "flung" it into the car with a swinging motion of my left arm. BIG mistake! I heard "pop, pop, pop!" and knew that I'd done some damage. Since we had to catch our flight, I took a couple of Ibuprofen and grabbed an ice bag for the cross-country trip. Once we arrived in California, my sister-in-law secured an appointment for me with her orthopedic doctor. A standard x-ray didn't reveal anything, but he suspected that I'd torn the rotator cuff. He recommended that I get an MRI when I got home, and gave me a shot of cortisone that provided some relief.

I returned to Orlando and went to the Jewett Orthopedic Clinic in Winter Park. When I described the sound that I heard while hoisting the bag, the doctor cringed – not a good sign. An MRI confirmed a torn rotator cuff in my left shoulder. Rest, pain medication, and physical therapy were his suggestions for treatment, with a caveat that this type of injury didn't usually heal by itself, and surgery may be necessary at some point. On a follow-up visit, the doctor noticed that my left hand was shaking. He commented that it might be a result of the trauma of the injury.

I had been diagnosed with sleep apnea a few years earlier and had consistently used a C-Pap machine each night to control snoring and maintain proper breathing. Sometime in October I had a routine follow up visit with my sleep doctor. During my examination, the doctor began to focus on my left hand. He asked me, "How long have you have that tremor?" I explained that I'd hurt my shoulder and that the shaking was a result of the injury. The doctor quite confidently stated, "I don't think it's related to your shoulder. That appears to be a Parkinson's tremor."

The doctor's pronouncement was quite a shock. One part of me wanted to simply reject it altogether. After all, this was not his area of expertise. However, this was a doctor I liked and trusted. Seeing the empathy in his eyes when shared his opinion led me to believe he just might be right. My practical side urged me to seek a second opinion. My emotional side whispered that my world was about to change.

My next move was to consult with my primary physician. She appeared to agree with the sleep doctor's assessment and promptly ordered a brain scan. Laura went with me because I tend to get claustrophobic in MRI machines. The sedative that they gave me helped, though I kept apologizing to the tech because my left hand was shaking throughout the procedure.

The results of the MRI were reviewed by my primary physician, who in turn referred me to a local neurologist, a specialist who could confirm my condition.

The initial exam with the neurologist included walking down the hallway, touching my index finger to his finger and several other fine motor skill exercises. Without any hesitation, he arrived at his diagnosis and informed me that I did, indeed, have Parkinson's disease. The date of the diagnosis was January 6,

2010. Ask any "Parkie" – a person living with Parkinson's – and they will know the date of their diagnosis by heart.

So many questions. What do I tell my family? What will my future hold? Will I be able to deal with this dramatic change to my life? What kind of a life will I have ahead of me?

PD Heroes

When I was first diagnosed with Parkinson's disease in 2010, I didn't know anyone personally who had the disease. Over the past seven years, I've had the good fortune to meet and become friends with several individuals who have dealt with Parkinson's on their own terms. They have chosen to "Live well" and to push back every day. I call them my "PD Heroes" because I look up to them for inspiration to keep moving along my own path, especially when times get tough.

The "typical profile" of a Parkinson's patient is age 60 and predominantly male. Having been diagnosed at age 58, I fall into that category. I have met both men and women who are around my age. I've also met a number of people who were diagnosed at a much earlier age as having "Young Onset Parkinson's disease." That can be quite a shock when someone is 50, 40, 30, or even younger.

Throughout this book, I will share stories about a number of people for whom I have a great deal of respect and admiration. Young or old, male or female; they are confronting PD with strength and dignity every day. When I occasionally find myself doing less than my best in terms of exercise and other areas which I know help in the battle against Parkinson's, I simply think about any of these people to get back on track.

CHAPTER 2

Learning About Parkinson's Disease

MY MIND WAS A BLUR as I left the neurologist's office. Parkinson's disease – the name, the "death sentence," kept rolling around in my mind. "Why did this disease pick me? What will happen to me? Did anyone else in our family ever have this before? Will I be able to work and provide for my family? How long do I have to live?" They were tough, scary questions with very few immediate answers.

The doctor had been quite clinical and matter-of-fact about his diagnosis. Other than writing out a prescription, he answered very few questions, or I was simply too stunned to present many logical questions at that point. It was more like, 'Good luck. Make an appointment with the receptionist at the desk. Don't let the door hit you on the way out." Thank you very much. That was the extent of my first visit with the pill pusher.

I'd probably been handed a couple of brochures when I left the neurologist's office and may or may not have read them. I may have Googled a few websites, but was cautious about "information overload" and becoming even more scared or confused by reading too much about symptoms, side effects, and treatment options.

The days and weeks came and went. Life went on. I began to relax a bit, realizing that I didn't feel much differently than I had prior to receiving the diagnosis. I began to ask myself a couple of more practical questions, "What exactly is this thing called Parkinson's disease?" and "What can I do about it?"

My knowledge of Parkinson's disease at that point would fit into a thimble. I knew that Muhammad Ali, Michael J. Fox, and Pope John Paul II each had this condition, and not much else.

Instead of getting too technical, I turned to someone whom I trusted for some insight – Michael J. Fox. Why this person? Well, quite frankly because I'd seen him grow up on TV, enjoyed his work in "Family Ties" and the "Back to the Future" movies, and been as shocked as the rest of the country when he boldly announced that he had been diagnosed with Parkinson's disease at an early age. He put a human face and a new perspective on what was widely considered to be an old person's disease.

My "extensive scientific research" consisted of listening to two of Michael J. Fox's audio books, "Lucky Man: A Memoir" (2003) and "Always Looking Up: The Adventures of an Incurable Optimist." (2010). Two quotes resonated with me. The first was, "You don't die from Parkinson's, you die with it." That put me at ease. This wasn't going to be something that would take me out right away, at least not like an inoperable form of cancer. The second quote was, "Parkinson's is a boutique disease." That means that it presents itself differently in each individual patient who contracts it. Armed with those two concepts, I decided to go with the basic premise, "kinda sucks," and chose to wait and see how this would all play out.

I've always been a believer in "signs." A few months after my diagnosis, during a business trip, I was changing planes between flights in Atlanta. On the wall of the train level, I saw a poster featuring Michael J. Fox. The quote on the sign was, "Determined to outfox Parkinson's. Optimism. Pass it on." Having an overabundance of optimism myself, I decided on the spot that this would all work out.

Still, it was important for me to know what I was dealing with and what the future may hold. So, what exactly is Parkinson's disease (PD)?

 In his documentary film, "Capturing Grace," filmmaker Dave Iverson offers the following dictionary definition of Parkinson's disease. "Parkinson's – a progressive, neurological disease, for which there is no cure." That certainly paints a bleak picture. He found that definition over forty years ago when his father was diagnosed. Since that time, his brother and then Dave, himself, went on to receive their own PD diagnoses. Dave says that the definition has not changed over the years. However, he says, "What has changed is our understanding of what it is to live with Parkinson's."

Dave's film, which is well worth watching, chronicles the "Dance for PD" program created by dance instructor David Leventhal at the Mark Morris Dance Group in Brooklyn. While the world of accomplished dancers and people challenged by the physical limitations by Parkinson's seem like polar opposites, this story demonstrates the "transformative power of art and the strength of the human spirit."

As a lifelong optimist, I grasp for nuggets of hope and tend to ignore bleak and limiting definitions such as the one above. Early on in my PD journey, I discovered the Davis Phinney Foundation, a nonprofit organization whose mission is to help people with Parkinson's to live well today. In fact, they popularized the concept of "living well" in the Parkinson's lexicon. The group was founded by Davis Phinney, an Olympic cyclist and the first American to win a stage of the Tour de France. He was diagnosed with Parkinson's disease at age 40. When his diagnosis derailed a television career as a bike racing analyst, he created a group that focuses on providing information, inspiration, and tools to people living with Parkinson's. The objective of the Foundation is to motivate them to take action to improve their quality of life right now. One resource that they provide is the *Every Victory Counts* manual, a detailed reference book jam-packed with information about Parkinson's disease and tools to help Parkinson's patients, their Care Partners and families to take control of their condition.

To provide a basic understanding of Parkinson's disease, the Davis Phinney Foundation has graciously granted me permission to reprint a section from their website entitled "Parkinson's 101." (© 2017 Davis Phinney Foundation for Parkinson's. Excerpted from www.davisphinneyfoundation.org with permission)

What is Parkinson's?

Parkinson's is a complex disease that can affect almost every part of the body, ranging from how you move to how you feel to how you think and process. While researchers have discovered certain genetic and environmental factors that seem to influence the development of Parkinson's, there is no single cause of Parkinson's or predictor of who will get it. Parkinson's is not life-threatening, but it is progressive, meaning symptoms and effects of Parkinson's get worse over time.

Parkinson's disease is a brain disorder associated with a loss of dopamine-producing nerve cells (neurons) deep inside the brain. Dopamine is a neurotransmitter (a chemical substance) that helps regulate the body's movement. Less dopamine in the brain means less control over movement and less mobility in general. Many treatments for Parkinson's work to replace or enhance lost dopamine.

Parkinson's is both chronic and progressive, which means symptoms will change and get worse as time goes on. The rate of progression will vary from person to person. While Parkinson's does not directly cause death, complications such as choking due to swallowing difficulties, pneumonia from aspirating food into the lungs or severe injury caused by falls that can come in the late stages of Parkinson's may lead to death.

Parkinson's is officially classified as a movement disorder because it involves damage to the areas of the brain, nerves and muscles that affect the speed, quality, fluency and ease of movement. While the effects of Parkinson's on movement are often the most visible symptoms, like tremor, other impacts of Parkinson's not related to movement, like emotional and cognitive challenges, can sometimes have an even greater effect on your quality of life.

No two people living with Parkinson's will experience symptoms or progression of the disease in the exact same way. Just because something is listed as a symptom of Parkinson's does not mean you will experience it.

Other non-motor symptoms of Parkinson's can include difficulties sleeping, trouble with executive functioning, like making a decision or packing a suitcase, mood changes that can bring depression, apathy, anxiety (or some combination of these), sleep problems and fatigue.

The more visible physical symptoms of Parkinson's, like tremors, slowness or stiffness, start in most people after 60-80% of certain dopamine-producing nerve cells are damaged. These symptoms are called motor symptoms. One of the main jobs dopamine-producing nerve cells have is controlling our movement, which includes the planning and initiation of movement. As these dopamine-producing neurons are lost, once routine everyday activities like walking and balance are affected.

Because Parkinson's is a chronic condition, your symptoms and available treatment options will change over time. Everyone's experience with Parkinson's is different, which can make anticipating the progression of symptoms frustrating.

Why do People get Parkinson's?

Parkinson's is second only to Alzheimer's as the most common neurodegenerative disease in the United States,affecting between 1 million to 1.5 million Americans. There are more people living with Parkinson's in the U.S. than the number of people living with multiple sclerosis, muscular dystrophy and Lou Gehrig's disease (ALS) combined.

An estimated 50,000 to 60,000 new cases of Parkinson's are reported annually in the U.S. alone. Between 7 and 10 million people are estimated to be living with Parkinson's around the world.

Most people living with Parkinson's are older than 65 and about 60 percent are male. About 1 in 100 people over the age of 60 have Parkinson's, while there are fewer than 1 in 1,000 people under the age of 50 living with Parkinson's. 15% of people with Parkinson's are under age 50 and only 5% are under age 40. Typically, individuals under the age of 50 and diagnosed with Parkinson's are referred to as having young onset Parkinson's (YOPD).

There is no known cause of Parkinson's, nor have scientists identified a set of characteristics that accurately predict if someone will develop Parkinson's. Discovering a biomarker, a biological characteristic that can predict if someone will develop a certain condition, is a current focus of ongoing research.

What Causes Parkinson's?

While researchers have discovered certain genetic and environmental factors that seem to influence the development of Parkinson's, there is no single cause of Parkinson's or predictor of who will get it.

The complexity of the brain has made the search for the underlying causes of Parkinson's difficult. While there is currently no known cause of Parkinson's, scientists and researchers believe a unique combination of genetics, environment, lifestyle and other factors are at play for each person who develops the disease. Some people with Parkinson's may have a genetic connection and will often have someone else in their family with Parkinson's. Others may point to specific environmental factors, such exposure to pesticides, or lifestyle factors, like head trauma, that they believe influenced their developing Parkinson's.How is Parkinson's Diagnosed?

Since no two cases of Parkinson's are ever exactly alike, Parkinson's can be very difficult to diagnose. Physicians determine you have Parkinson's after reviewing your medical history, self-reported symptoms and a clinical examination conducted by a neurologist or a movement disorder specialist.

Since doctors diagnose other medical conditions using sophisticated technology, many are surprised to learn a Parkinson's diagnosis is based on your medical history and a simple examination. While your healthcare provider may take other steps, such as order blood and urine tests, check copper levels and order a brain scan, such as an MRI or CT or Dastan that measures dopamine, these tests do not diagnose Parkinson's disease. They are used to either confirm the diagnosis or determine if another medical condition is causing your symptoms."

(© 2017 Davis Phinney Foundation for Parkinson's. Excerpted from www.davisphinneyfoundation.org with permission)

In my case, the primary symptoms were a tremor in my left hand, micrographia (my handwriting was getting smaller and beginning to look like my grandmother's), a decreased arm swing and a slight dragging of my left foot. None of this was particularly painful, and initially this combination of symptoms didn't limit my regular daily activity to any great degree.

I never spent a great deal of time trying to figure out how I had contracted Parkinson's. It didn't appear to be genetic since I could not recall anyone else in my family who had been diagnosed with it. The other major cause is often listed as environmental. Other than putting weed killer on the lawn, I'd never worked with hazardous materials in the past. I determined early on that my time was better spent learning ways to control or slow the progression of the disease rather than focusing on how it chose me.

My neurologist prescribed a low dosage of a couple of basic medications that had proved effective in treating Parkinson's. They did help to control the tremor reasonably, which was the most observable symptom to others. I was open about my diagnosis to my family, close friends, and my employer. Everyone seemed to be fairly understanding. I didn't want to attract unnecessary attention to my condition, so I was pleased that the medications provided some relief.

For the first time, I thoroughly read the entire warning label that came with the drugs I had been prescribed. I wanted to be certain that I followed "the rules." One warning that caught my attention was to essentially not eat any type of cheese. While I was willing to follow the instructions precisely, that seemed rather excessive and a radical change to my normal diet. I picked up the phone and called the pharmaceutical company's customer support line. They acknowledged that the restrictions about cheese were contained in their product advisory to patients, however they told me that a requirement when they first launched the product about ten years ago, as part of their efforts to gain approval from the FDA. They informed me that further testing had shown no adverse effects from eating cheese, only suggesting to avoid particularly strong types such as Gorgonzola. That was a relief, but it did demonstrate that I needed to become my own advocate and ask a lot of questions about any form of treatment.

Once I discovered that I could still have pizza, I relaxed a bit. It was hard to tell which of the multitude of symptoms that I might get in my individual version of Parkinson's, so I didn't dwell on that unknown. For the time being, I focused on controlling the combination of symptoms I knew about at that moment. My priority was providing for my family, keeping a positive outlook, and paying closer attention to my overall health. I decided that the "inconvenience" of Parkinson's was something that I would have to fit in around the important priorities in my life.

I began to consider ways to improve my overall health. I had enjoyed riding a bike ever since I was very young. I'd gotten away from that hobby and started thinking about taking it up again.

PD Heroes – Davis Phinney Foundation – Boulder, CO

John with Davis Phinney

I was very fortunate to discover the Davis Phinney Foundation early on in my PD Journey. This group was created by Davis Phinney, an Olympic Bronze Medalist. He had a remarkable professional cycling career, which included becoming the first American to win a stage of the Tour de France, and is recognized as the winningest American cyclist of all time. When he reached the end of his riding career, he had the next stage of his life all planned – working as a television cycling commentator. Life being what it is sometimes, just as he began to transition from pedaling to calling races, he was diagnosed with Parkinson's at age forty.

After taking some time off to adjust to his diagnosis, Davis decided to create a foundation that focused on helping

18

people with Parkinson's and their Care Partners to "Live Well Today." When I discovered his organization, I knew that his philosophy aligned well with my core values. It has been an honor to get to know Davis, his remarkable staff, and to represent his foundation as an ambassador.

The Phinney family truly has cycling in their blood. Davis' wife, Connie Carpenter Phinney, earned a gold medal in the Los Angeles Olympics. Their son, Taylor Phinney, is currently a professional cyclist. I particularly appreciated a story written about Taylor on a challenging day on the pro circuit. Entitled, "This is not a story about last place," the article recounts a day when Taylor experienced a couple of flat tires and a broken chain. He wasn't hanging with the front riders. However, rather than just drop out, which many other riders were doing, he pushed on. His motivation that day was thinking about how his father deals with the burden of Parkinson's disease. Taylor said, "I knew that if my dad could be in my shoes for one day – if all he had to do was struggle on a bike for six hours, but be healthy and fully functional – he would be me on that day in a heartbeat." Taylor Phinney said, "Every time I wanted to quit, every time I wanted to cry, I thought about that." The apple doesn't fall far from the tree in this family.

CHAPTER 3

Getting Fit Might Be a Good Idea

LIKE MOST ADULTS, I HADN'T RIDDEN a bike in years. During a vacation to Mackinac Island in 2006, I rented a beach cruiser and took an eight-mile ride around the perimeter of the island. No cars are allowed on the island, so I felt perfectly safe, and thoroughly enjoyed the pleasant scenery all around me.

After returning home, I researched bikes and selected an Electra Townie 7D. It's not an electric bike. The Electra Bicycle Company is the manufacturer of this hybrid/comfort bicycle. In addition to being sturdy and allowing me sit more upright, it included a feature that appealed to me called "flat foot technology." That feature allows the rider to put their feet on the ground when stopped. I took it out for a spin now and then around the neighborhood. Unfortunately, the bike stayed in the garage most of the time.

One decision that I'd reached after my Parkinson's diagnosis was to take better care of myself, lose some weight, and attempt to get into shape. I'd dropped about twenty pounds already while going through physical therapy for the torn rotator cuff in my left shoulder. The shoulder was much improved, so I began spending a bit more time on my bike. That was fun, until I crashed. I was riding on the local trail one day, and while attempting to make a sharp turn onto a narrow bridge I smacked my shoulder into a steel guard rail. Naturally that was the one that I'd been rehabbing for the past few months. I kept my bike upright, however my garage door opener flew out of my basket and landed at the bottom of the creek.

I told my neurologist about the accident. I also shared the fact that narrow sidewalks made me uncomfortable. He said that some people with Parkinson's have perception issues. His recommendation was to limit my cycling to a stationary bike in a gym. I thanked him for his advice and left the office. Before I reached my car, a response formed my mind: "Bullshit!"

The crash was not caused by my disease, it was simply a combination of a poorly designed approach to the bridge and operator error. I had been riding my bike too fast to properly navigate the sharp turn. I immediately dismissed the good doctor's advice and simply used more caution during my future rides.

I shared the story of my mishap with a friend who was familiar with bike safety. After reviewing photos that I'd taken of the bridge, this person agreed that the bridge needed some attention to make it safer for all cyclists. The official trail was about twelve feet wide, however the bridge section was only about three feet – the original distance before the surrounding sidewalk had been widened to qualify as trail-worthy. He suggested that I contact a person he'd met at a cycling conference named Mighk Wilson, a Bicycle and Pedestrian Planner with the MetroPlan Orlando.

I shared the information about the crash and photos of the bridge with Mighk Wilson. He was very empathetic, however he suggested that I report the design flaws to the appropriate authorities in Seminole County where I lived. I followed up and they made some improvements. I added Mighk as a friend on Facebook. Little did I know that he would be extending an invitation to me later that year that would change my life.

PD Heroes – Jimmy Choi – Chicago, IL

Receiving a diagnosis of Parkinson's at age 27 was a bitter pill to swallow for Jimmy Choi. He had been an athlete in school, married his high-school sweetheart (Cherryl), and owned four restaurants in Chicago. Diagnosed in 2003, just four years later he needed a cane to help him walk, gained a lot of weight, and had to sell his restaurants. In 2010, Jimmy underwent an experimental brain surgery that involved stem cell therapy replacement. He wasn't certain that he got the "good stuff," but he was able to throw away the cane the day after the operation. Friends began to encourage him to take walks, then to jog a bit, and he soon completed his first 5K event.

In 2012, Jimmy completed his first marathon in Chicago. Since then, he has run twelve more, including the New York City Marathon and the Walt Disney World Marathons. In fact, when he runs at Disney, he takes part in an event called the "Dopey Challenge" which consists of four races over four days – a 5K, 10K, Half Marathon, and Full Marathon. In 2016, Jimmy fell during a training run a few days before heading to Orlando and separated his shoulder. Most people would have withdrawn from the event. Not Jimmy, he completed the four races with his arm in a sling.

Jimmy is also a cyclist. As I mentioned earlier, I had the good fortune of meeting him at the 2015 Parkinson's Unity Ride in Las Vegas where he rode with the front group most of the way. In 2016, Jimmy took on a challenging ride in Chicago called "Sub 5." It was a 100-mile bike ride with the goal of finishing in under five hours. With the help of some dedicated friends who created a mini-peloton to assist him, Jimmy completed that ride in under five hours, with four whole minutes to spare. Later he said that he couldn't feel his right leg for the last fifteen miles of the ride, but kept pushing on with only his left leg.

In addition to his intense athletic accomplishments, Jimmy has been a huge supporter of Team Fox, the fundraising arm of the Michael J. Fox Foundation. Jimmy and Cherryl founded an annual event in Chicago called the "Shake It Off 5K." Now in its third year, they attract over 500 runners and raise over $25,000 per year. That alone earns them an invitation to the Michael J. Fox VIP dinner each year in New York City. But it's Jimmy's humility and ability to create awareness about Parkinson's that earned him a seat next to Michael J. Fox at one of the recent dinners.

Jimmy works hard to stay ahead of his Parkinson's disease. He does all this for his wife, Cherryl, and his two kids, Karina and Mason. I am honored to know him and humbled to call him my friend.

In July 2017, Jimmy Choi appeared on the show *American Ninja Warrior.* The episode was taped in Kansas City when he competed in the qualifying round there. While Jimmy fell off the "split logs" challenge into the water, he brought a tremendous amount of focus and attention to the Parkinson's Community. In fact, the amount of air time that he received in teaser ads leading up to the actual program probably did more to create awareness about PD than all of the money spent by the major Parkinson's organizations for a full year combined. Michael J. Fox taped a video of words of encouragement. Jimmy will be back next year to compete, stronger than ever.

Please consider taking part as a virtual runner in his annual Shake It Off 5K. He always shares really cool "bling" with all participants.

Jimmy Choi's annual fundraiser can be found at www.shakeitoff5k.com.

CHAPTER 4

Cycling Savvy

THE OLD EXPRESSION "JUST LIKE RIDING A BIKE" is often used to describe something that comes second nature and should be easy to do. It implies that we already know everything about an activity and can take off where we left off. When it comes to actually driving a bike, that couldn't be further from the truth. We can always learn more and continuously improve our skills.

As a kid, I loved zipping around on my bike and was very proud when I saved up enough money to buy twin newspaper baskets, which made me an entrepreneur. In college I was fearless, easily navigating 4-inch bike trails through the woods from the dorm to class. As an adult, I didn't put in much time at all on my bike. For the most part, the Electra Townie remained comfortably parked in the garage. At the beginning of 2010 I finally followed through and dropped 30 pounds by using a treadmill, but that was boring. I finally dusted off my bike and began riding once again. Portions of the Cross-Seminole Trail run near my house, so I began to take advantage of the fun of short rides.

I continued to follow Mighk Wilson's Facebook posts about a bike-handling class that he and Keri Caffrey had created. After reviewing the information on the Cycling Savvy Course, I decided to invest some time and energy into the program to improve my skills and give myself more confidence. The training consists of a four-hour classroom session, followed the next morning with a bike skills session called "Train Your Bike," and finally a ride around town to experience real-world cycling techniques. That ride portion was called "Tour of Orlando" (or the location in which the class is taking place).

I signed up for the November 2010 Cycling Savvy session. Even though I was 59 years old at the time, I was nervous as I entered the room and wondered if I was out of my league. Everyone from the instructors to my fellow classmates made me feel included and welcome. I quickly learned that the group consisted of a variety of ages and skill levels, and immediately began to relax.

Right out of the gate, Mighk and Keri opened our eyes to several myths about bike riding and their new vision for safe and effective two-wheeled transportation, which applies equally well to both the novice and the daily urban bike commuter. They supported their case with well-prepared videos and animations to demonstrate each aspect of this technical portion of the program. As a trainer myself, I could clearly see that they had found a way to break through to the adult learner. My classmates and I were not only being informed, but were being challenged to rethink what we knew about cycling. It was exhilarating to realize that we were being empowered to lead the dance out on the road.

Anxious to begin the actual riding portion of the training, I checked in before the designated start time the next morning. I had checked my tire pressure on my bike the night before, so I was shocked when I removed my bike from the car rack to find I had a flat tire. One of my classmates immediately sprang into action and patched the flat but it didn't hold. Mighk kindly loaned me a tube to use and informed me that the inner band on the wheel had deteriorated and was allowing the end of one of the spokes to pierce the tube. I followed his advice and promptly folded up a dollar bill to cover the errant piece of metal. Although slightly embarrassed that I'd held up the group for a few minutes, I felt a sense of camaraderie with both my trainers and classmates. They weren't going to leave anyone behind. This was going to be fun.

And fun it was! Though not always easy. The three-hour bike handling skills portion took place in a large, open parking lot. Each drill was carefully designed to improve our comfort, confidence, and command over our "vehicle" – our bikes. Snail races, using gears for quick acceleration, super slow tight turns, balancing after stopping, shoulder checks, and evasive snap drills led to high-speed turns and emergency stops. The "building blocks" all came together by the end of the morning, with each of us now possessing a "tool bag" of essential bike-handling skills.

We had ridden several miles crisscrossing that parking lot. Next on the agenda was lunch. Only one thing was standing between us and a tasty burrito – navigating down Maguire Road and turning onto Colonial Drive, crossing three lanes of traffic and executing a left-hand turn onto Primrose Ave.

ARE YOU CRAZY????? Looking at the busy road with cars whizzing by brought back images of a game of Frogger. Between the faith that we'd placed in our instructors and the new-found confidence that we had in our individual ability, the class ventured out and successfully and flawlessly completed that first "feature" as a group. Collectively, we mustered our confidence and realized, "We can do this!" After getting the first exercise under our belt, we celebrated with a collective high-five. It was a glorious moment. Hooray!

The afternoon was spent analyzing and facing down several other "features," or learning opportunities. Our trainers mapped out the plan with colorful chalk on the pavement, explained both the hazards and the best approach that would ensure ease and safety. This experiential form of training was perfect for adult learners. We weren't being lectured by our instructors. We weren't being given some meaningless test. We were part of the learning process and the success of everyone in the class was just as important to us as our own small victories. We rode together between exercises, but were given the opportunity to personally experience each feature on our own. From riding through a roundabout to learning the proper way to cross diagonal railroad tracks, to seamlessly "controlling" the center lane on Princeton Street to avoid the Interstate-4 on-ramp, to navigating the fearsome Ivanhoe Interchange (not once, not twice, but three times); each exercise brought us a new level of confidence.

After making our way through the construction near the new Arena, we had to cross the bridge over I-4 on Anderson. That climb was a challenge. I downshifted so far that there was only one gear left – my internal "Little Engine That Could Gear." I dug deep and made it to the top and was immediately rewarded with a swift ride down the other side. I learned a lot about my bike that day too – after cresting that hill, Keri rode up next to me and said, "Yeah, your Townie is great for stopping, not so much for climbing" and then told me she was proud of me for toughing out the climb up that hill. At that point of the day, my competence and confidence were soaring. I wasn't going to fall behind my classmates in any way.

One of the reasons I took the Cycling Savvy Course was that I had begun to feel uncomfortable riding on sidewalks to get to the trail in my area. I learned that there were plenty of good reasons to feel that way – uneven and broken sections of sidewalk, the need to steer around pedestrians and other bikes, the possibility of a wheel getting caught between the sidewalk and deeply edged grass, which could lead to a fall, and the higher risk of being hit by a car. I had feared that my balance was an issue. By going through the course, I had plenty of opportunities to disprove that assumption and build my skills. As we were riding in a group at the end of the day, I was carrying on a great conversation with one of my classmates about ocean cruises that we had each taken. It dawned on me that I was riding side by side with him just a shoulder width apart and tracking exactly one wheel length behind the rider in front of me – and I was perfectly relaxed, comfortable and having a blast. This program helped me to realize the freedom and fun that comes with being in command of your own bike. I was a kid again!

The support and inspiration that Mighk and Keri provided had been tremendous. Keri had my back while we were riding the final leg back to the parking lot during the class. While riding along, I felt my wedding ring slip off my finger. Using a skill that I had learned that morning, I turned around in the saddle and told her that my ring had fallen off. She said, "I know, I just rode over it." She promptly went back and retrieved the now "flattened" ring. If she hadn't trapped it under her wheel, it might have rolled off into a gutter. Nice save! I later had the ring repaired and continue to wear it.

Cycling Savvy Class

After we returned to our starting point and took a group photo, I shared one little detail with Mighk and Keri. That was the fact that I had been diagnosed with Parkinson's disease at the beginning of the year. The tremors were not that obvious at that point, so neither of them had noticed my hand shaking during the day. I assured them that I wouldn't have put them, my classmates, or myself at risk if I hadn't felt confident that I could complete all the requirements of the class. I thanked them for designing such a useful course and for encouraging me throughout the day. I felt that we would stay in touch and ride again together as a result of this experience.

PD Heroes – Tim Hague, Sr. – Winnipeg, Canada

In 2010, Tim Hague, Sr. noticed a tremor in his left foot, the first signal that he had Parkinson's disease. He was formally diagnosed in 2011. Tim had cared for people living with Parkinson's in his career as a registered nurse. His adoptive father also had PD. Tim continued leading a healthy lifestyle and encouraging physical activity among other people with Parkinson's due to his belief that exercise has significant positive impact on the progression of the disease.

Tim's wife, Sheryl, encouraged him to apply for the first season of Amazing Race Canada. Having followed the US version for years, she was convinced that he would at least get an interview, telling Tim that they'd never had anyone on the show with Parkinson's before. He applied, with his son, Tim Jr., as his teammate. Not only did they get the interview, they were chosen to be on the show, and they won! Throughout the race, they were error-prone and often lost, however they persevered and came out on top.

Tim now spends his time speaking to large and small groups, sharing his message, "Live Your Best." His core concept is wrapped up in the idea of "having the strength to do your best, the courage to be content with what your best produces, and the will to persevere." From the Amazing Race Canada, he learned one important lesson, "Just stay in the race."

The Davis Phinney Foundation has invited Tim to address Victory Summits in Malaysia, Florida, and California. He is one of the most inspiring motivational speakers I have ever heard. His website contains a TED talk and links to the Amazing Race Canada. It can be found at www.timrsr.ca

CHAPTER 5

Hooked on Riding

CYCLING SAVVY HAD BEEN A TERRIFIC learning experience, a confidence builder, and a lot of fun. Afterwards, I felt very motivated to practice my new-found bike-handling skills. I live in Lake Mary, Florida which is located about 20 miles north of Orlando. There are a couple of decent trails in my area – the Cross-Seminole Trail and the Seminole Wekeiva Springs Trail. I prefer the second one because it winds through the woods and is longer – perfect for training rides. The problem is that the Seminole Wekeiva Trail is located on the other side of Interstate 4. While there is a pedestrian/bike bridge across I-4, a rider must travel several miles out of the way to access it. The more direct route across the freeway is Lake Mary Boulevard, a six-lane major interchange.

As intimidating as the six-lane road appeared, I felt that it could be managed with the skills that I had learned in the class. I wrote to Keri Caffrey, explained the challenge, and told her that I thought that I could manage it. Rather than simply saying, "Go for it," Keri came up to Lake Mary to help me analyze a solution for getting across the freeway. She brought her laptop, which was loaded with satellite images of the bridge and a route that she had worked out to get us safely across a very complex and

busy road. That may sound like overkill, but it sure beats ending up like a bug on a windshield.

Cycling Savvy taught me that I could ride a bike again. Now I wanted to put the skills that I learned together and spread my wings, beginning by crossing I-4.

Keri videotaped the ride and wrote a detailed article about it afterwards for the Commute Orlando website. Here is her description of the event:

> From Keri Caffrey's article "Problem-solving a massive, high-speed, car-centric interchange"
>
> "A week after taking the November 12-13 Cycling Savvy Weekend course, John Alexander sent me an email asking what was the best way to ride over the Lake Mary Blvd/I-4 interchange. Most people (including experienced road cyclists) regard that interchange as impossible for a cyclist. But John didn't. He wrote, "I 'analyzed' the drive-up Lake Mary Blvd. across I-4 and said to myself, 'I could ride that!'"
>
> It's true! John learned and experienced all the basic components for driving his bike across this interchange in Cycling Savvy."

Rather than simply telling me to "Go forth, apply the skills that I had learned, and hope for the best, Keri came up with a plan and completed the ride with me. She also took video of the event, using both forward- and rear-facing cameras on her bike helmet.

She presented me with several options and allowed me to take part in deciding our best route after hearing the pros and cons of each one. We lined up with four lanes of traffic on Lake Emma Road prior to turning westbound on Lake Mary Boulevard. The other cars passed us quickly and we had 30 seconds of silence with the road just to ourselves. Another platoon of cars caught up with us. Despite being highly visible, one driver in a BMW came up behind us rather quickly and honked his horn, then passed and cut directly in front of me. I saw him in my mirror and anticipated his aggressive behavior. Once he passed, we were able to maneuver to complete a left turn at the next light with no problem.

Returning eastbound went just as smoothly. At the end of the route, Keri declared, "All in all, it was a perfect ride."

The video from the ride has been shown to every Cycling Savvy Class since we completed the ride that day as an example of what can be accomplished with proper skills and advance planning.

Completing that ride was a real boost to my confidence. I knew that I could evaluate a situation and apply the skills that I had learned to safely travel just about anywhere on my bike. I was becoming drawn into this bike riding culture, whether for my own personal enjoyment or riding with others.

First Friday Rides

A tradition of the Commute Orlando and Cycling Savvy groups is to take part in a "First Friday Ride" each month. The ride begins near the Orlando Science Center at Loch Haven Park. The group varies in size from a dozen to over twenty riders. One of the goals is to demonstrate to local motorists that cyclists can actually be "civil," which is demonstrated by the fact that the riders follow the rules of the road, come to a full stop at red lights, and signal for all turns. The concept of "We Are Traffic" is clearly communicated.

Before each ride, the group leaders explain the rules to everyone since there are often new riders in attendance. Helmets are required. Depending on the time of year, headlights and tail lights are also mandatory. The group travels two abreast, except for sections with mandatory bike lanes. The leader in the front sets the pace, generally about 10 – 12 miles per hour. That is a comfortable pace for all riders. It is a social ride and not intended to be a race. The route is about ten miles and takes place around the perimeter of downtown Orlando. If traveling on a four-lane road, the group stays in the right-hand lane unless they are setting up to make a turn at an upcoming traffic light. The leader will signal that a turn is planned and everyone behind passes back that command. Another leader is stationed at the back of the pack and they determine when it is safe for the group to move over. A command comes up from the rear to "take the lane" and the group smoothly and safely merges over to the inside lane.

From my very first "First Friday Ride," I felt comfortable being part of the group. My Cycling Savvy class had taught me the basic skills required to ride in close proximity to other riders, to signal my plans to slow down or stop, and to courteously point out hazards in the road.

Most importantly, the First Friday Rides were a great social experience. They gave me a chance to chat with others while riding at a comfortable pace. Being from the suburbs, I didn't know that much about downtown Orlando. The rides gave me an opportunity to learn about the city and discover new restaurants, since the group often stopped for a drink or a meal after completing the circuit.

I met a number of people through the First Friday Rides. One evening I was riding next to a gentleman named Charles Badger. He told me that he was an "ultra-distance cyclist." Asking him to define that, he said that he would go out and ride 200 miles (or more) over a weekend. Charles wasn't bragging about the distance that he rode, simply stating a fact. While I didn't immediately aspire to begin riding such distances, it did open my eyes to the fact that a person could travel quite a way by bike if they put their mind to it. I didn't see Charles for some time after that ride, but our conversation made me wonder just how far I could push myself and what type of goals I might choose to pursue. Perhaps my first goal should be riding 200 miles, in total, since taking the Cycling Savvy class.

Holiday Light Ride

I suddenly saw opportunities to ride everywhere. The New Hope for Kids organization offers an organized Holiday Light Ride each year. It's quite festive and upbeat. This group provides support for children who have lost parents at an early age, something that I could relate to personally. Not only was this an opportunity to log a few miles, it was also a chance to meet people and support a worthy cause.

Everyone decorates their bikes, so I purchased some battery-powered lights, along with a light-up snowflake, and even added a monkey light to my wheel rims, which displays illuminated images, such as Christmas trees, when the wheels spin.

Keri and another Cycling Savvy instructor, Lisa Walker, were serving as marshals for the ride, so they were at the front of the pack. I settled into a spot in the middle of the group and soon realized that many of these riders didn't share the same rules of the road that I'd learned in Cycling Savvy. As we made the first turn, a teenager fell and took out several others with her. Fortunately, I'd learned to anticipate just such a situation and didn't get tangled up with the group. Instead, I stopped and guided others around the wreck. That prevented further collisions. Everyone was fine and we all continued on our way to the cookies and hot cocoa at the end of the ride.

I took part in that ride the next couple of years, even serving as a marshal myself to help keep everyone safe. One year, my daughter, Jen, and her husband, Bob, rode along. I was one proud "Grampy," pulling my granddaughter, Lilly, in the baby trailer. We even added lights to the trailer. My wife, Laura, helped pass out cookies during the midpoint of the ride. Those were festive events, enjoyed by both the riders and the homeowners who proudly showed off their holiday decorations and enjoyed watching the decorated bikes pass through their neighborhood.

Riding Solo

At first I wasn't that focused on amassing miles, but when I began to hear about some of the distances that others had ridden, I found it both fun and interesting to track my results. This also gave me a way to measure whether I was challenging myself and getting stronger.

I discovered a phone app called Cyclemeter for keeping track of my cycling miles. It provides some interesting information – miles ridden, total time, elevation gained, fastest speed achieved, average speed, etc. I then transfer that information to dailymile.com. That site shows visual tracking of my results and can be viewed by day, week, month, and longer.

Riding on the trails in my area, I settled into a ten-mile loop as a standard "training run." Initially, it was difficult to complete even that distance. I would get winded easily and have to stop frequently to rest. Was this caused in part by Parkinson's disease, or simply due to being out of shape? I don't know, but I kept on riding that route on a regular basis. The more I rode, the easier it became and the faster I could complete the circuit. While I live in Florida and it's quite flat, my route had a bit of a decline on the way out. That meant that I had a slight incline on the return. I remember the day when I finally completed the entire return without having to drop down from my highest gear. I felt that I had accomplished a great deal in terms of my cycling stamina when I reached that point.

Riding by yourself also allows for some quiet time. My time spent riding along the Seminole Wekeiva Trail became a form of meditation. Sometimes I mulled over some of the questions that had concerned me when I was first diagnosed. Mainly, I enjoyed the scenery and felt a sense of accomplishment.

I wasn't setting any land speed records, but I was enjoying being active. It also helped my efforts to continue to lose weight. In addition, I had begun reading about the benefits of exercise for people with Parkinson's. I knew that riding made me feel better and gave me the energy that I needed to do my job, which included quite a bit of travel. Most of all, it was fun!

41

PD Heroes –Ken Tripp – Louisville, KY

Ken Tripp with his motorcycle escort unit traveling through Cincinnati

I happened across Ken Tripp on Facebook as he was preparing for a 500-mile bike ride from Louisville, KY to Cleveland, OH. We connected right away due to several common factors. We both had lived with PD for about the same time, we were close to the same age, both had been trainers in our professional careers, and both rode Catrikes.

Ken had decided to do his ride to raise funds for Team Fox and the Davis Phinney Foundation. It was interesting to read his blogs as he prepared for his ride. Ken's wife, Kathy, would be driving their SUV as a support vehicle. About half of the trip would be on trails, but much of it would be along roads. He contacted the police department in Cincinnati about providing an escort through the busiest parts of that town. They obliged by providing six motorcycle police officers who rode with him for about twenty-six miles.

Despite long days of riding, Ken posted a summary online at the end of each day. It was thrilling to read the last blog when he reached his final destination, the Rock & Roll Hall of Fame in Cleveland.

Ken is also a very accomplished photographer and continues to go on sunrise photo shoots on a regular basis. Due to his Parkinson's, he takes most of his handheld pictures now on his iPhone rather than using one of his collection of top-quality cameras, due to the stabilization feature.

I speak frequently with Ken and we compare notes about the progression of our PD, nutrition, cycling, and our mutual interest in travel, particularly taking our wives on Viking River Cruises. Ken and Kathy have been gracious hosts during visits that I've made to Louisville a couple of times. On my last trip, Ken and I toured the Muhammad Ali Center, which was quite informative, especially for two Parkies.

CHAPTER 6

Sharing the Joys of Cycling

DISCOVERING SOMETHING NEW IS SPECIAL and interesting, but sharing that experience with others is exhilarating and memorable. That's how getting involved with cycling has been for me. I participated in several group rides throughout the Orlando area and made new friends along the way. I gained confidence in "driving my bike" and that has allowed me to feel comfortable riding whenever and wherever I desire. I had the pleasure of sharing my new-found love of cycling with friends who were visiting from far flung parts of the world.

I met Roger Barr in 2005 at the Central Florida Scottish Highland Games. As soon as he started talking, I realized that he wasn't from "around here." In fact, Roger and his wife, Margaret, live in Scotland, near Glasgow. We struck up a friendship based on mutual interests in Scottish heritage. My wife, Laura, and I visited the Barrs in Scotland in 2006. We've kept in touch, and when they mentioned that they were coming to America for a month, I hatched a plan to drag Roger along on a "wee bike ride." He owns a bike at home and I knew that he would be up for the idea.

Roger is one of fewer than 4,000 people who have climbed all 283 Munros (defined as a mountain in Scotland over 3,000 feet.). That basically took a lifetime. In addition, he has hiked the entire distance of the Pennine Way, a 267-mile trail extending from Scotland to England. In June of 2011 he had plans to complete the Coast to Coast Walk, 190 miles across England, much of it on mountain ridges. So, I figured that the "Sweet Ride" sponsored by Commute Orlando and the Bike/Walk Central Florida groups would be a piece of cake for him. In addition, I talked Reg Lyle into joining us. Reg is the Pipe Major for the Rosie O'Grady Highlanders Pipe and Drum Band and played at my daughter's wedding rehearsal dinner in 2007 and Roger's son's wedding in Scotland in 2008 – it was quite an honor for an American to be invited to play in the homeland. Reg has some serious cycling experience as well, having ridden from Cincinnati, Ohio to New Orleans, LA a few years ago.

The Sweet Ride took place on Friday, March 18th. It was a perfect spring evening. A Commute Orlando friend helped me out by loaning not one, but two bikes – one for Roger, one for Reg. Once the adjustments were made, the group was off for a tour around Orlando, finally arriving at Delish Yogurt Shop in Baldwin Park. Our wives – Laura Alexander, Margaret Barr, and Jo-Ellen Lyle – didn't take part in the ride but met us to celebrate our accomplishment. Roger said several times, "This is marvelous to be riding around town as a group." However, while savoring his dessert, he realized that we still had four miles to ride to get back to the car. While he had the legs for the 14-mile ride, he decided that he would primarily stick with walking and climbing since his "bum" was a bit sore. I was excited to celebrate reaching my goal of riding 200 miles since my Cycling Savvy Class in November.

Shipboard Spin Class

A couple of days after the Sweet Ride, Roger, Margaret, Laura, and I set sail on the Norwegian Dawn for a five-day cruise to the Western Caribbean, with stops in Grand Cayman and Cozumel. I took an onboard spin class – a first for me. The legs held up well, but I was surprised at how much pressure it put on the shoulders and upper body. My shoulders had been tender for a while due to my torn rotator cuff, so I only took the one class, but it was a blast to be pedaling at full tilt watching the deep blue Caribbean pass by. I even thought of renting a bike in Grand Cayman, but two reasons held me back – being a British Colony, they drive on the left, and all the drivers I observed were insane. Not a good combination. Cozumel didn't appear to be any safer, so no international riding for me.

After our return from the cruise, Roger and I took another 10.5-mile ride along the Seminole Wekeiva Trail. I was pleased to show it off to my friend. We combined the ride with a bit of "geocaching," a popular treasure-hunting activity using GPS coordinates. Roger was a seasoned Geocacher and I'd been wanting to learn about it. I identified several potential locations along the trail and we set out. Stopping to search for the hidden treasures makes a ride more relaxed. We successfully found three containers – a "nano," which is similar to a 35mm film canister hidden in a rock, a magnetic box placed under a bench, and an ammo box with other small treasures left by others. A fourth site eluded us; that I'll have to track down another day. Sharing these rides with my good friend from across the pond was a highlight of our visit. It was during that bike ride that I first suggested to Roger that he take me to the top of a Scottish Munro.

First Friday Ride – Almost!

After a week out of town on business, I woke up back at home on Friday morning a bit stiff from the seven hours cooped up in airplanes. I forced myself to do my morning stretches to work out the kinks, because I was determined to take part in the First Friday that evening. The day went quickly as I played catch-up from being away all week. I kept checking the weather report and it didn't look good. Around 5:00 p.m. I texted the ride organizers to ask if the First Friday ride was still on. It was still a go. However, if it was pouring at the start time, those who showed up would seek shelter and enjoy a beer together.

Not wanting to miss out, I loaded up the bike on my car rack for the drive from Lake Mary to Lock Haven Park in Orlando. As soon as I started up the car, I noticed that the engine felt rough. Driving out of my neighborhood, there was a high-pitched noise coming from the engine compartment. I got about a mile from the house and was waiting in a left turn lane when the car flat-out died. I still had battery power, so I could turn on the hazard lights. I could begin motioning drivers to go around me since I couldn't move the car at all.

I went down my mental checklist – call AAA, call the local mechanic, call home, call the First Friday ride group. Check, check, check, and check. All set, just needed to wait for the tow truck. Interesting to observe humanity when you are "broken down." Basically, most people treat you like you are the biggest inconvenience of their day. Even though I had my emergency hazard lights on, many drivers still pulled up right behind me, honked when I didn't move when the light changed, and honked again after backing up and finally passing. I finally got out of the car and used my lime green neon "Commute Orlando" shirt to get people's attention and spent my time waiting by directing traffic. There were several people who were kind enough to stop and ask if I needed help or a jump. I thanked each of them and told them that AAA was on the way.

About 30 seconds before the tow truck arrived, a Seminole County Deputy pulled up. He jumped out of the car and instead of asking me, "Can I help you?" or "What's the problem?" he said, "You can't be here" – as if I had chosen to have my car stall on purpose. Right at that moment, the AAA truck swooped in and had me hooked up and ready to go. So, "Adios Officer!" and I jumped into the cab of the truck for the ride to the mechanic. Turns out that the tow truck driver was a mountain bike enthusiast. He said that he missed the hills in Pennsylvania. I suggested that he check out the meetup.com site for some adventurous rides in this area. You never know where you're going to run into good people.

After unloading the car, I put on my helmet, windbreaker, and bright green shirt and headed for home. Very handy to have a bike with you when you must abandon your motor vehicle. Also, a good thing to only be four to five miles from home.

I took the Cross-Seminole Trail. That route felt safe, even though it was pitch black out. My lights helped, but I would have liked to have had a stronger headlight. I was surprised to come upon several people walking on the trail in the dark. There was even a group of teenagers sitting in the middle of the trail. They were all dressed entirely in dark clothes. After nearly running over them, I was much more cautious.

Since I had to go past Bruster's Ice Cream along my route, I stopped and picked up a pint of mint chocolate chip to make up for the evening's inconvenience. That, along with some Thin Mint cookies that I'd purchased from a friend did the trick.

I finished up the ride home on the streets, owning the lane and riding big – just like I'd learned in Cycling Savvy. Although the road was almost completely deserted, I still was honked at, but I felt fine anyway. After all, even though I'd missed out on the official First Friday group ride, I did get to ride my bike that Friday evening. Bike riding just puts a smile on my face. Despite the challenges, I felt that I'd come out ahead.

Where to Next?

Part of the joy of cycling is not knowing where your next ride will take you or who you might meet along the way. However, planning still plays a crucial role. I've certainly learned that exploring new places by bicycle is a lot of fun and very rewarding – and quite simply, a joy-filled experience. Planning a route allows you to visualize what the ride will be like. There are quite a few resources to draw upon for ideas and suggestions, including your local bike shop (or one in the town that you plan to visit), local riders, or cycling websites that help riders share knowledge of good bicycle routes. If you plan to ride on the road, take a course like Cycling Savvy first to build your skills and confidence.

Finally, find some people to accompany you on your rides. They may hail from places as far away as California or Scotland, but the experience is so much better when it's shared with good friends. Mention your interest in cycling to co-workers, neighbors, and others in your circle. You'll be surprised how many ride or would like to take it up. You can see so much more and appreciate the area around you when traveling on a bike and in the company of your friends. Get out there and ride!

PD Heroes – Tonya Hills Walker – Winter Park, FL

Tonya is a wife, a mother, a law professor, and a fashion blogger. She was diagnosed with Young Onset Parkinson's at age 34. The effect on her life was significant. Over time, however, she has regained control by having two Deep Brain Stimulation surgeries and resuming activities that she previously enjoyed, such as running. Recently she took up boxing and has found that it improves her cognitive alertness, her balance, and causes a decrease in her rigidity.

I met Tonya at a Young Onset PD meeting in Orlando and have always been impressed with her courage and confidence. She was chosen to represent the Parkinson's More Than Motion group at the World Parkinson's Congress in Portland in 2016. She shared her story at their booth and created awareness about younger people living with this disease. It was a treat to spend time with Tonya, her husband Chad, and their son Chase at that event.

Tonya has always been fashion conscious. She has a blog called the Shoe Maven. In its introduction, she tells of having to give up her high heels after her diagnosis. However, following her DBS surgeries she was able to regain much of her balance and return to wearing her beloved high heels. She has raised money for the Michael J. Fox Foundation through an annual event in Orlando called The Art of Fashion and last year hosted an international social media campaign called Heels On, Head Up! to raise awareness for young onset PD. Her website is www.theshoemaven.com.

CHAPTER 7

Freedom to Ride

IN THE SPRING OF 2011 I TRAVELED to San Diego for a business conference. One morning I found myself with some free time. I'd noticed quite a few bike commuters and relatively light traffic in downtown San Diego, so I started investigating bike rentals. It occurred to me that a great place to ride would be just across the San Diego Bay in the small town of Coronado. I couldn't have been more right.

Googling bike rentals, I had decided on "Bikes and Beyond," which is located near the Coronado Ferry Landing, which also is the home to several shops and restaurants. Arriving a bit early, I walked around, grabbed a coffee and sat on a bench enjoying the view of downtown San Diego across the bay. At precisely 9:00 a.m. I picked up my bike from Tom, who was working the bike shop that day. He provided a great map and explained optional routes to the primary one suggested.

Tom set me up with an Electra seven-speed as my rental, which included a bike lock and helmet. This model was very similar to my bike at home.

The route that I followed started along a trail which followed the bay heading south. Soon I passed through Coronado Tidelands Park. Even though I had only been riding for less than ten minutes, I had to stop when I spotted a unique stainless steel bicycle sculpture atop a pole about 50 feet up in the air. It is a kinetic sculpture entitled "My Bike." It measures 17 feet high and 10 feet long. The wheels are 40 inches in diameter. The entire bike moves around about the pole and the wheels turn. The rider has long stainless steel "locks" of hair blowing behind. The overall effect, to me, represented the freedom of riding a bike in the most carefree manner. I later learned that the artist was Amos Robinson. I appreciated him placing such an interesting work directly in my path. It was the first time I took an unplanned stop on this ride around Coronado, and I'm glad I did.

I rode on with a smile on my face and followed a course that took me right to the Hotel Del Coronado.

The Hotel Del Coronado was originally built in 1888. It has survived all these years and grown over time through numerous re-models. The hotel has played host to count-less celebrities and several US Presidents. The movie *Some Like It Hot* with Marilyn Monroe, Tony Curtis, and Jack Lemmon was filmed there in 1959. Walking through the lobby feels like step-ping back in time. For my Floridian friends, the Grand Floridian Hotel at Walt Disneyworld is styled after this stately old prop-erty. I took some time from the ride, locked up my bike and walked around the property, enjoying the lobby, the landscap-ing, the chef's vegetable and herb gardens, and the views of the Pacific Ocean.

Back on the bike, I passed several beautiful homes and continued along a route that was almost free of traffic. I was having fun taking photos of some of the homes and their unique architec-tural features. As I passed one house with a vine-covered arch-way to the side, I said to myself, "I wish I'd taken a photo of that." Then it dawned on me – I'm on a bike and can easily stop and turn around. That was the second unplanned pause during this ride.

I biked past the entrance to the Naval Air Station North Island – one of the eight facilities that makes up the Naval Base Coro-nado. Naturally this is a restricted area. It takes up about two-thirds of the upper Coronado peninsula. Much of the community is made up of military and support personnel from the base, so there were signs in front of many of the houses that I passed stating "Home of a Naval Aviator." This is also the home of two aircraft carriers, the USS Carl Vinson and the USS Ronald Reagan. Across the bay in San Diego is the USS Midway – now a permanent museum which I had the opportunity to tour that evening as part of the conference.

Turning south, I headed back towards Bikes and Beyond. Along the way, I stopped to chat with a gentleman walking his dog. Turns out he was a retired music teacher, so we talked about music education for a while. He asked if I'd recently moved to the area, but I told him that I was just visiting. Coronado would be a great place to live, especially since it was so bike friendly, so I took it as a compliment that he thought I might be a local. That was the third time that I pulled over during my ride around this small city. Taking the few extra moments to enjoy the bike sculpture, take photos of the houses, and talk to the "music man" enhanced my ride a great deal. It dawned on me that I could have only done these things because I was riding on a bicycle. A phrase popped into my head: "Bike Speed." The meaning refers to the fact that one can go as fast or as slow as they wish on a bike. That became the name of a blog that I created.

I returned the bike and drove back to the convention center, arriving with all of five minutes to spare before the afternoon exhibit hours started. The ride was a lot of fun and I'm very glad I made the time to fit it in. It was a highlight of my trip. I doubt that I would have had the confidence to go out and rent a bike in an unfamiliar city if I hadn't taken the Cycling Savvy course.

San Antonio – The Alamo and More

On another business trip, I carved out some time for an afternoon bike rental. I found a shop called Alamo Bike Rental and was outfitted with a comfortable cruiser to use to explore the downtown area.

Naturally, my first destination was The Alamo. It was originally known as Mission San Antonio de Valero. It was founded in the 18th century as a Roman Catholic Mission and was the site of the Battle of the Alamo in 1836. Fortunately, The Alamo was restored over the years and provides a great deal of insight into Texas history. I had visited in the past, but it was fun to arrive by bike and take a leisurely walk through the exhibits and enjoy the history of this site.

The bike shop had also suggested that I take a ride through the King William Historic District. This part of town dates back to the 1790's when the land once belonged to the Mission. In the 1860's, the area was divided into lots and sectioned by present-day streets. Soon after, German nationals who immigrated to Texas began to settle in the area. Large and impressive homes were constructed in Greek Revival, Victorian, and Italianate styles. Many of the houses fell into disrepair by the end of the Second World War, but the area was revitalized in the 1970's and is now listed on the National Registry of Historic Places. I had been to San Antonio several times before, but the freedom to roam gave me the opportunity to take in this special part of town, enjoy the architecture and learn a bit more about the history of the area.

Fitting short bike rides into business trips was allowing me to continue to build up my cycling miles, provide exercise and offer relaxation along the way. Reducing stress is important for controlling Parkinson's symptoms, so this was just what the doctor ordered.

PD Heroes – Allie Topperwein – Columbus, TX

2014 was not a great year for Allison Topperwein. In August, she separated from her husband and was divorced two and a half months later. On New Year's Eve that same year, she was diagnosed with Parkinson's disease at 37 years old. As a newly single mom, she had a choice to make. She woke up on New Year's Day 2015 and told herself, "This is not how my story will end." Soon she began writing a blog called "Lit Within" and created a nonprofit by the same name to help women of all walks of life overcome whatever obstacles stand in their way. She's certainly helping men to do the same thing.

Early on, Allie learned that "exercise is the only thing proven to slow the progression of Parkinson's disease." In November 2015, she signed up for a mud run, which involved a seven-mile run and 25 obstacles. She finished 4th in her age group and in the top 13% overall against more than 1,400 competitors,

The next "logical" step was to try out for "American Ninja Warrior." She only trained for four months but was selected by the show to compete at the Oklahoma City taping of the program. On June 20, 2016, she stood at the starting line ready to begin, with a thunderous roar coming from the audience – both there and at home. The first obstacle she faced is known as the "Quintuple Steps." Competitors must jump back and forth between the steps that are built at a sharp angle and risk sliding off them and falling into the water. After reaching the last step, the contestant must leap forward, grab a rope, and swing to land on a platform. Allie cautiously maneuvered through the first four steps. When she landed on the last step, she began to slip. Using every ounce of energy in her being, she clawed her way back to the top of the step and pulled herself up, saving her right to jump for the rope. After several attempts, she slid off the rope and into the water. I can say that I, along with many viewers across the country, was cheering her on every second that she was on the course. I don't think I've ever seen anyone put so much fight and heart into their effort. And, of course, she'll be back to compete again. Allie's driving force is to be strong for her young daughter, and to raise her daughter to also be strong. I had the privilege of meeting Allie at the World Parkinson's Congress in Portland in September, 2016. She is just as sweet as she is strong and fierce.

CHAPTER 8

Opportunity Presents Itself

THROUGHOUT THE SPRING OF 2011, I continued to participate in First Friday Rides and other social cycling events. While I enjoyed my time on the bike and the pleasure of getting to know more people, I didn't spend a lot of time thinking about the impact that this might be having on my Parkinson's disease. My symptoms continued to remain well under control with my medication, but I probably hadn't given a sufficient amount of credit to the increase in my exercise level. I was having too much fun riding, with the side benefit of losing some weight in the process.

Unlikely Patient Rides a Bike

Occasionally, I come across articles or videos online about exercise and Parkinson's. I pay particular attention to those that mention cycling and its effects on PD. One remarkable video from the Netherlands showed a gentleman who had lived with Parkinson's for ten years. The patient was experiencing a great deal of "freezing" – a condition that only allowed him to walk a few steps before falling. The man explained to the doctor that he exercised regularly. In fact, he said that he was a cyclist. He told his doctor that just the day before he had ridden his bicycle about 10 kilometers (six miles) and that he rides his bicycle for miles and miles every day. The doctor had his doubts, so they took the patient out to the parking lot, helped him onto a bicycle, and watched him pedal around at ease. Apparently, the brain might use different areas for controlling activities such as walking and cycling. A before-and-after video was made to record this transformation, and it is amazing to watch. This gentleman could barely walk, and yet he has the ability to ride a bike effortlessly. The YouTube link is here: https://youtu.be/aaY3gz5tJSk

While I had not encountered any difficulty with my walking up to that point, I still found it intriguing that there might be a positive connection between exercise and controlling some symptoms of Parkinson's disease.

Forced Exercise Bicycle Study

I came across another article about a study by Dr. Jay Alberts of the Cleveland Clinic. He had always been an avid cyclist and regularly took part in an event called RAGBRAI (Registers' Annual Great Bicycle Ride Across Iowa.) The route changes each year, but it averages about 500 miles and takes seven days to complete. Dr. Alberts was planning to do the ride one year with some friends. One of these was a woman who had Parkinson's. She was 41 years old and in good physical condition, and fully capable of doing the ride. The woman and her husband had decided to use a tandem bike instead of their individual road bikes that they normally used. The problem was that they hadn't practiced on the tandem prior to the big ride. Within a mile of the start, they realized that their lack of training and lack of coordination was a big mistake. If they continued, it may have led to a divorce. Dr. Alberts offered to ride the front position on the bike, with the woman riding behind him. Her husband would use Jay's road bike. Before they started, he told his "passenger" that he wasn't going to cut her any slack. He knew that she could keep up with his pace due to her level of fitness.

The woman struggled a bit at first, but managed to keep up and enjoy the ride. Jay rode at his regular pace, which required the woman to exert a bit more than she might have on her own. Halfway through the week, she commented that she "didn't feel like she had it (Parkinson's)", as several of her symptoms had temporarily disappeared. At the beginning of the week, Dr. Alberts had observed the woman filling out some forms and noticed that her handwriting was atrocious. This wasn't a surprise, since many people with Parkinson's display a condition called micrographia or small, illegible writing. At the end of the week, Jay saw her writing out a birthday card for a friend and her handwriting looked like calligraphy. Dr. Alberts was just as amazed with this change as the woman was herself. When he returned to work, he established a formal study to evaluate the effects of "forced rate activity" on several Parkinson's patients. The conclusion was that the "forced rate bicycle exercise" appeared to be an effective therapy for Parkinson's disease. This is not a cure, but it does clearly demonstrate the importance of exercising at a quick tempo on a regular basis.

The positive correlation between cycling and Parkinson's symptoms improvement coming out of Dr. Albert's study has led to the establishment of "Pedaling for Parkinson's Spin Classes" taught at YMCAs across the country. In my area, a fellow person with Parkinson's named Howie Apple leads a class of about 30 other "Parkies" three days a week. Howie's speech is soft, a symptom of his Parkinson's, so others call out the cadence and other encouragement. In addition to a great workout, it is also an excellent form of socializing. I have taken Howie's class a few times and find it a lot of fun and very invigorating.

Dr. Albert's work is proof that aggressive exercise is just as important as medicine for controlling some of the symptoms of Parkinson's disease.

Ride With Larry Trailer

At some point in the spring of 2011, Keri Caffrey sent me a link to a movie trailer for a documentary that was being developed called *Ride With Larry*. The filmmakers were raising funds for the project through Kickstarter. They were seeking $50,000 to finance the documentary. The subject of the film was a 64-year-old gentleman named Larry Smith. He had been a police captain in Connecticut and was diagnosed with Parkinson's disease at age 42. Being a responsible individual, Larry knew that he had to retire from his profession in law enforcement. Their fallback position was to find a community where his wife, Betty, could pursue a tenure track as a university professor. They uprooted their two young children and moved their family to Vermillion, South Dakota. In the summer of 2010, Larry told Betty that he wanted to do something big before it was too late. At first, he considered the lofty goal of riding across America. Betty suggested throttling that back a little bit. So, Larry instead elected to ride across South Dakota – approximately 300 miles from the top to bottom of the state.

Larry and Betty's niece, Katie Skow Villarreal, and her husband, Ricardo, were documentary filmmakers. Friends had suggested that they make a film about her uncle Larry for their next project. Ricardo would serve as the film's co-director, along with his friend Andrew Rubin. Andrew's father also had Parkinson's disease. Andrew's brother, Matthew, served as the film's other producer, along with Katie. They filmed interviews and scenes of Larry riding his bike around Vermillion during the fall of 2010 and shared that video on the internet as part of a Kickstarter project to raise funds for the actual film. Their Kickstarter goal was $50,000, but they were fortunate to raise over $67,000 due to the strong interest in the topic.

In the trailer, Larry shared his philosophy that "If you love life, you'll fight for it." He put a call out for others to come to South Dakota and join him in crossing the finish line on June 25, 2011. His adventure would span 300 miles in five days, with the final day being a ride from Sioux Falls to Larry's home in Vermillion. That call to action genuinely struck a chord with me. I said to myself, "I have to do this!"

I knew that I didn't want to do this by myself, so I called my son, Brian, who lives in Los Angeles. I asked, "How would you like to come to South Dakota in June to ride bikes with Dad?"

Without asking for any details, he immediately said, "Yes." After five minutes I called him back and asked, "Do you even own a bike?" He did not, so I sent him money to buy one to begin training during the remaining couple of months before the ride.

I began to think through the logistics to make this happen. The first decision was whether to fly or drive to South Dakota. It's a 1,600 mile drive from my home near Orlando, FL to Sioux Falls, SD. That would take almost 24 hours of drive time. The one advantage with driving would be that I could bring along my own bike. My bike is known as a hybrid or comfort bike. It is not the

65

best design for a long-distance ride, but it is comfortable for me. It allows me to sit more upright and avoid putting too much pressure on my hands and wrists. If I wanted to fly and ship my bike, that would entail the extra expenses of having it packed into a special bike box by a bicycle shop and paying an extra baggage fee to the airline.

Then I began exploring options for renting bikes. After making a few calls, I found Harlan's Bike and Tour in Sioux Falls. I was pleased to learn that they stocked Electra Bicycles. As a bonus, I would be able to rent one with 21 gears, an improvement over the 7 gears available on my own Electra Townie. At least I wouldn't have to get used to a different bike in an unfamiliar area. I also placed a rental order for a Bianchi for Brian. All that I would need to bring would be my helmet, bike gloves, and bike shoes. I felt much more comfortable having secured a decent ride for this big adventure.

Airline reservations, hotel accommodations, and car rental were all easy to accomplish. Actually getting to Sioux Falls would take a bit of time since it required three separate flights to get there.

Once the travel plans and bike rentals had been organized, my focus shifted to preparing for the ride itself by getting out on my bike and training. Most of that would involve regular rides on the Seminole Wekeiva Trail. Naturally, Florida is flat, but my normal ten-mile route had a bit of a grade on the southbound run, which meant that I had to build up some stamina for the climb out on the northbound return. That became easier week after week. I then added additional miles each week, but knew that I had to test out my ability on a longer ride, the West Orange Trail.

PD Heroes – Allison Smith – "The Perky Parkie" – Laguna Niguel, CA

Talk about getting a raw deal, Allison Smith was diagnosed with colon cancer at age 24. She endured 14 surgeries in a three-year period. Surviving that, you would think that you would have earned a "free pass" from other illnesses until you were like 90 years old. Nope, at the ripe old age of 32, she was diagnosed with Young Onset Parkinson's disease. What are the odds? Too high to calculate.

Most people would roll over at that point, but not Allison. She wrote a book about her experience entitled "I Am Not Contagious" and started a blog for the Parkinson's Community under the name "The Perky Parkie." Most of the time, her posts are funny, other times not so much as she addresses the challenges of dealing with a degenerative disease at such a young age.

In 2010, she launched a program called "Parkinson's In Balance." The idea was to offer fitness classes, support groups and community events at no cost. She said, "I would have never asked for this life, but I wouldn't change it for a thing. I have made amazing friends and found the meaning of my life... helping others." Her uplifting blogs have helped many a Parkie maintain a sense of humor and balance in their own lives.

I finally had the opportunity to meet The Perky Parkie in person at the Victory Summit in Las Vegas in 2015 and again at the World Parkinson Congress in 2016. She's as fun and energetic in person as she is in her blog articles. I was disappointed, however, that she didn't have her puppy sidekick, Crash, along at either of those events. Apparently, he's not given the freedom to travel like Allison.

Allison's blog can be found at: www.parkinsonsinbalance.net

CHAPTER 9

West Orange Trail
Training Ride

ONE OF THE GOALS OF TACKLING the West Orange Trail was to
"test my mettle." The definition of mettle is "a person's ability to
cope well with difficulties or to face a demanding situation in a
spirited and resilient way." I needed to complete a longer ride to
determine just how well-prepared I was for the 65-mile route
that I would be attempting to complete in South Dakota. The
West Orange Trail was 45 miles, so that would be an adequate
test of my skills.

The West Orange Trail is popular – and populated – with riders
of all skill levels, from novices on rentals, to families riding together, to flat-out racers. Even with heavy usage, however, the
groups spread out quickly so it never feels congested. It is well-
maintained with full-service support buildings called "stations"
and limited service outposts with water and restrooms spaced
along the way. We started at mile marker zero at the Killarney
Station, which houses a complete bike shop.

Rodney Youngblood joined me for the ride. He is a Cycling Savvy Instructor and, as I learned, a very patient person. We crossed a restored railroad bridge that spans the Florida Turnpike, passed the Oakland Nature Preserve and rode around the Oakland Outpost. Shortly after that we rolled past the xeriscape and butterfly garden. When we arrived at downtown Winter Garden around mile five, the route guided us onto a median along Plant Street, which doubled as a park with fountains and benches. We had to slow quite a bit since this was a popular area for families enjoying their Saturday morning.

We took the spur that runs down to the Clarcona Horsepark and were entertained by the riders on horseback practicing their dressage routines. It was a nice hill down to the horse park and a slow climb back to reconnect with the main trail. The section from mile 13.5 north to Apopka was the least favorite of the day. Parts of it are in full sun for long distances – that sapped the energy from both of us. The south side of Apopka runs through some very disadvantaged areas, but the kids in the area enjoyed waving at us as we rolled by and they got a kick out of my ringing my bike bell.

Our next pit stop was the Apopka Station. Rodney was pleased to see that they had a full-service bike shop since he had broken a spoke on his bike. While it was still rideable, his bike was giving off a screaming sound liked he was choking a canary. He removed his rear wheel and took it in, only to find that they didn't stock his specific size of spoke. After a few adjustments, we were back on the road and the canary was muffled for a while. The trail goes down a fairly steep hill that was fun to ride down, with a slow crawl up the back side of Apopka High School. From there the "trail" – simply meaning a wide sidewalk – goes along Park Avenue and then crosses Welch Road. It ends rather unceremoniously a couple hundred yards down from a McDonald's. That meant that we'd reached our midpoint for the day with 22.5 miles showing on the bike odometer.

We could have returned exactly the same way we came, but remembering the fun hill – and the consequences of having to ride back up it – I suggested that we simply take the flat route and ride straight down Park Ave. Since Rodney commutes daily to his job at Orlando International Airport, this four-lane road with moderate Saturday afternoon traffic was a piece of cake for him. He lined up in a queue behind five cars exiting the Post Office at a light and I planned to join him as he went past. I didn't get going in time, so I had to wait for the next light. It was invigorating to control my lane for the couple of blocks that it took to catch up to him. It's always a treat to watch traffic smoothly change lanes behind you with no horns honking. Well, there was one guy who hung behind me, then came up beside me, rolled down the passenger window and said, "According to Florida Bicycle Statutes, you aren't allowed to take up the whole road."

I simply waved, but was amused by the fact that I was in my lane and he was in his – by no means was I "taking up the whole road," simply controlling the right-hand lane – and, in fact, sharing that lane with Rodney. By the way, he had a bike rack on the back of his car!

That encounter was balanced out during our last rest break back at Chapin Station. A dad was taking his seven-year old daughter  for a bike ride. They were clearly having fun being outdoors and spending time together. The dad was asking us if we'd seen any deer along the trail, apparently anxious to show his daughter some wildlife. We had to confess to only seeing a few squirrels and egrets. He then asked if we had a bike pump. We were taking a well-deserved rest, sitting in a pair of rocking chairs on the porch of the station, but we gladly pulled ourselves up and proceeded to pump up his tires. Turns out he had a brand-new bike – in fact, the tag from the store was still hanging off the handlebar. The front tire was almost completely flat, so after pumping that up we proceeded to inflate the rear as well. The "ABC mantra" (air, brakes, chain) was running through my head from my Cycling Savvy class, but instead of "lecturing" the gentleman in front of his daughter I simply handed him a brochure and suggested that he consider attending a class to improve the riding experience for both he and his daughter. It was a refreshing moment after a long day on the trail.

We stopped on the way back at a bench to enjoy a delicious lunch – as in PB&J sandwiches. While I had eaten a good breakfast, I'd only had a few handfuls of peanuts during other breaks. The sandwich recharged me, but I probably should have had another later in the ride because I did begin to run out of steam towards the end. In fact, I began calculating our time and realized that we'd been riding for quite a while. I am able to do my "standard" ride on the Seminole Wekeiva Trail in an hour flat, which is averaging 10 miles per hour. Excluding breaks, we were well below that pace – hence the reason that I said earlier that Rodney was very patient with me. Some of this was due to encountering more hills than I'm accustomed to, part to less than adequate nutrition, part to my personal level of conditioning, and part to the fact that I simply have a heavy bike.

Around mile 35 it dawned on me that my objective of taking on the full 65-mile ride in South Dakota might be a tall order and that I may have to opt for the 30-mile route, especially since the group may be traveling at a faster pace than I was capable of doing. I do have the heart, soul, and spirit and am quite resilient – however, I do have limitations. I decided that I had to at least attempt the 65-mile route. Having my son, Brian, along for the ride would make the day all that much more special.

We arrived back at Killarney Station about 3:35 p.m. – six and a half hours on the trail, with about five and a half hours in the saddle. I did stay well-hydrated, which was critical considering that the thermometer registered over 93 degrees. I started with a full 70 oz. Camelbak and refilled it two times. As we passed the Oakland Station, I poured a spare water bottle into the hydration system, which was enough to get me the last three miles. Mine was the only car in the overflow lot and very few cars were remaining in the main lot. However, the bike shop was still open and we gladly purchased an ice-cold Gatorade to drink in celebration. My goal for the day had been to "run the full West Orange." I accomplished that distance and a bit more to spare. Final number on the bike computer for the day – 45.17 miles! If someone had told me last November that I would cover that great a distance in a week, much less a day, I wouldn't have believed it. In addition, I got to spend time with a great guy and appreciated Rodney's guidance, encouragement, and patience. I'd be proud to ride the trail with him again one day.

I was sure that I'd have quite a tale to tell after completing the Ride With Larry. I knew that it would be a special day – no matter the distance covered. I was still committed to completing the 65-mile route, and officially signed up to do just that.

There was one more decision to make prior to heading to Sioux Falls. All my riding up to this point had been done wearing tennis shoes and using the standard pedals on my bike. I had spoken with other riders and read up on "clipless pedals." This mechanism allows a rider to engage a cleat on the bottom of their shoe into a matching pedal. Once connected, each pedal stroke becomes more efficient. I had noticed with my own riding that my left leg wasn't quite as strong as my right. Using this type of pedal would force both legs to work at an equal level in both the down stroke and up stroke for a much more consistent ride.

It seemed that everyone told me the same thing about "clipless" pedals, "you will fall while learning how to use them." Well, falling was not an option. The torn rotator cuff in my left shoulder had healed well, but I didn't want to take a chance of reinjuring it. I decided to go ahead with the new pedals, but wanted to do it properly. When I had the pedals installed at a bike shop, I practiced "clipping in" and "clipping out" while riding on my bike on a rolling trainer. It seemed simple enough. Then I practiced in my own neighborhood with my son-in-law serving as my spotter. He had to catch me several times before I got the hang of engaging and disengaging from the pedals properly. With the training that I'd done, I'm not sure if I officially qualified as a cyclist but I had at least become a bicycle rider.

PD Heroes – Alison Sheltrown – Grand Rapids, MI

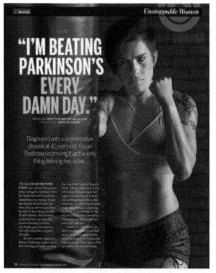

A pain in her right shoulder was the first indication that something was wrong. Diagnosed in 2014 at age 41, Alison was surprised, especially since she knew of few women or people her age who had Parkinson's. She made a couple of core decisions right away. One was that you can't stop living your life. She says, "Your life doesn't end. You have a different life." She's always led a healthy lifestyle, and soon came to realize that "Exercise is the only thing proven to slow the progression. It's not optional. It's a requirement."

She is a regular at the gym working out, lifting weights, and boxing (a popular sport for people with Parkinson's.) Through these activities, Alison is committed to making every effort to control the disease.

She also feels that it's important to connect with people and share what she has learned with others. She does that one-on-one by meeting with others who have been recently diagnosed, particularly Young Onset patients.

Alison is also very open and authentic in the posts that she places on Facebook. Recently she wrote about a bit of a setback.

"Real Talk:

I've become complacent.

I've been off my exercise routine.

I have been lax in my diet, not fueling my body the way I need to.

I've let my disease become a crutch. It slipped in slowly, sneakily.

I haven't been the role model I've aspired to be.

I've let my disease define me. Instead of me defining IT.

I've been stuck. But, I WILL get unstuck.

I know that I am STRONG, and I WILL get back on track.

I REFUSE to give up.

It starts NOW.

#iamstrongerthanparkinsons"

For me, a PD Hero isn't always the person who wins the race, but the genuine person who stumbles, gets up, and carries on despite the odds. I appreciate Alison's honesty and her tenacity.

CHAPTER 10

Ride With Larry

THE DAY BEFORE I WAS TO LEAVE for South Dakota I received a call from Harlan's Bike and Tour in Sioux Falls. The voice on the phone said, "We're calling to talk to you about your bike rental." My heart sank. What could be the problem? I was instantly convinced that they didn't have the Electra Townie that they had promised me and I would have to settle for a mountain bike or road bike that I wasn't familiar with riding. I asked him what the problem was. He said, "We don't have the 21-speed Electra Townie that you requested in our rental bike rotation right now. So, we're going to break a brand new one out of the box tonight and build it for you. It will be ready by the time you arrive tomorrow." That was a huge omen that this was going to be an outstanding adventure.

I flew to Sioux Falls on Friday, June 24th. Brian flew in from Los Angeles. After picking up our rental car, we drove over to Harlan's Bike and Tour to pick up our rental bikes. I had brought along my own pedals to ensure that they were properly adjusted for my bike shoe cleats. The mechanics swapped those out with the ones on the rental bike. They made sure that both of our bikes were set up properly and we were comfortable with everything. Once we had the bikes loaded in the car, the mechanics waved goodbye and one of them said, "Boy, that hill coming out of the park tomorrow where you start off is a doozy." I wasn't sure exactly what he meant, but I figured that we'd find out in the morning. His comment brought back my concern about being up to the task of riding the hills in South Dakota, but at this point there was no turning back.

We drove over to the park to take the bikes for a test ride along the river. The path was flat and the ride was smooth. No indication of the special hill that the bike shop guy had mentioned.

After checking into our hotel, we headed over to the Senior Center, the gathering place for the end of Day 4 for the Ride With Larry core group of riders. At the end of each day, even after riding 75 miles, they met with a local Parkinson's Support Group and shared their story. They encouraged the people with Parkinson's and their Care Partners to exercise and continue their fight against this disease by staying active. This was one of the first times that I had been with a large gathering of people with Parkinson's. I had not attended local support group meetings back home up to this point, mainly because they took place during the day and conflicted with my work schedule. It was a bit shocking to see many individuals who moved very slowly, had obvious tremors and facial masking. Even though I may have been the same age as several in the group, I felt much younger and more in control of my movement at that point.

When I had the chance to meet Larry Smith in person, I discovered that he was very soft-spoken. I had to lean in closely to hear him. However, I quickly learned that he has a quick wit and very dry sense of humor. I told him that I had trained for this event by riding 500 miles over six months. He replied, "Who's counting?" He wasn't making fun of me, simply grounding me.

One of the sponsors of the ride was the Davis Phinney Foundation for Parkinson's. This group was founded by Olympic cyclist Davis Phinney after he was diagnosed with Young Onset Parkinson's at age 40. The group's mission is to help people with Parkinson's to "Live Well Today." I had spoken with Program Manager, Ally Ley, prior to coming to South Dakota. It was a treat to meet this wonderful young woman in person. She had brought along bike jerseys from their organization for Brian and myself as a thank you for funds that I had raised prior to the ride. With her bubbly personality, she truly was a great representative for the Foundation.

The mayor of Sioux Falls presented Larry with the keys to the city, joking that it's not often that Sioux Falls bestows that honor on someone from Vermillion. He very sincerely, however, welled up with tears when he spoke of Larry's accomplishment, since the mayor's own father-in-law also suffered from Parkinson's.

Not only is Larry a member of his community, he has also been their baker for several years. When Larry and Betty moved to Vermillion, he continued with a tradition of baking bread that he had begun years before. The demand became so great that the local grocery store carved out an area that became Mr. Smith's Bakery. His talent was recognized in 2003 when Oprah Winfrey named it the "best bread in America."

Larry and Betty kept up their hiking and bike riding during the early stages of his Parkinson's disease. Over the years, Larry's balance had declined as a symptom of Parkinson's, and he had begun falling off his two-wheeled bike. A family friend, Steve Feimer, introduced Larry to a three-wheeled recumbent bike manufactured by a company called Catrike, which is based in Orlando, FL.

A highlight of the gathering in Sioux Falls was my chance to take a Catrike for a test drive. The company was a sponsor of Ride With Larry and he was riding one of their Expedition models. The Catrike gave him the security to ride wherever he chose to go. It had already carried him many miles this week.

The team from Harlan's Bike and Tour had brought along several Catrikes and were allowing people to try them out. I took one for a spin around the parking lot and found it to be a lot of fun, and very nimble. A particularly moving moment took place when a gentleman encouraged his 75-year-old wife to try one. She had Parkinson's and had facial masking, a condition where the muscles in the face cause the person to display little or no expression. Many people think that the person is sad or angry, however it is simply the inability to smile or display feelings. The woman was hesitant at first, but sat down on the Catrike with the help of the bike mechanics. They showed her where to place her feet and how to turn and apply the brakes. She started off slowly and gradually picked up speed as she made her way gently around the parking lot. As she returned to the starting point, she broke into a huge smile. Her husband broke into tears, saying that his wife hadn't smiled in years! It was a glorious moment for all.

PD Heroes – Friends for Phinney – Louisville, CO

Some of my PD Heroes don't actually have Parkinson's disease, but show a tremendous amount of support for the cause.

Kevin Cartin, Rick Baker, and Tom Casey attended Boulder High School together at the same time as

Davis Phinney. They followed Davis Phinney's cycling career as he went on to compete in the Coors Classic, Tour de France, and the Olympics. They were impressed that their classmate had more wins than any other American cyclist, but have been even more impressed with the way he now lives each day of his life with Parkinson's.

They began taking part in Victory Crew events in 2006. Kevin's wife, Kathleen Donohue, joined the group and they took part in the Copper Triangle ride that year. They've been doing that every year since.

In 2013, the group decided to take on a slightly larger challenge: to ride across the country from Oceanside, California to New York City. 100% of the funds that they raised for the ride were dedicated to the Davis Phinney Foundation.

They began the Friends for Phinney Coast-to-Coast Ride on July 20, 2013 by putting their rear wheel tires in the Pacific Ocean and finished 42 days later in New York City, dipping their front wheel tires in the Atlantic Ocean. In addition to averaging about 85 miles per day, they frequently met with Parkinson's support groups to share the message of "Living Well Today." They rode through heat, rain, mountains, prairies, and every other type of weather and scenery that could be found along the way. They posted their adventure on Facebook, and Kevin Cartin wrote a blog post each day after completing the ride and meet-and-greet.

Consistent with their tradition of participating in the Copper Triangle, the group made sure to arrive in Copper Mountain, Colorado along the way to take part in that 78-mile ride, climbing over three mountain passes over 10,000 feet as a side route just for fun. The riders seemed happy as they made their way across the country, as long as they had their daily ration of peanut butter and jelly sandwiches plus a steady intake of pickles.

I followed the group's ride from the very beginning. I was tempted to meet up with them along the way, but couldn't coordinate the logistics. As they were approaching Ohio, I contacted Kathleen Donohue and made arrangements for them to meet up with my brother, Chuck Alexander, as they were traveling through Ohio. Chuck set up a dinner at a long-standing local restaurant called Smitty's Place in Elyria, Ohio. The four riders were joined by Amy Collette, Tom's wife who was driving the support van for that week. Doug Bahniuk and his wife, Alissa, also took part, as Doug had cycled with the group that day. Doug is a member of the Victory Crew, and despite living with Parkinson's has completed cross-country bike rides, plus a 900-mile unsupported ride in Alaska. Word has it that the group devoured nine orders of Smitty's famous deep-fried pickles!

It's the support of people like this that make it possible for the Davis Phinney Foundation to provide education, information and hope to the Parkinson's Community. Their "leg power" not only took them across the country, but put *Every Victory Counts* manuals into the hands of many people. That book is considered a go-to tool for addressing questions about Parkinson's, helping people with PD and their Care Partners to prepare for their doctor's appointments and monitor their symptoms. It's a valuable resource which the Foundation provides at no cost. Find the manual and other valuable PD resources at davisphinneyfoundation.org.

Saturday – June 25, 2011 – Sioux Falls, SD

The morning of the big ride had arrived. It was a beautiful morning, crystal clear with a brilliant blue sky. It was quite a sight to see all the riders converge and unload their bikes. Larry Smith had begun the week accompanied by about a dozen close friends and family members. For this final day, there were over 100 cyclists assembled. I was excited to be there with my son at my side. We posed for photos and chatted with new friends from the night before, such as Caroline Theiss-Aird, one of Betty Smith's sisters.

The guest of honor arrived and said hello to a few people and called for his bike. Once he sat down on it, he was ready to go and the group began to roll out of Yankton Trails Park. Up front, leading the pack and gliding effortlessly around the first turn was Larry Smith – a 62-year-old, 20-year Parkinson's survivor, who had already ridden over 240 miles over the past four days on his Catrike – and he was moving along like his hair was on fire!

Brian and I joined the peloton, making the turn onto the road that the locals at the bike shop had described as a "doozy."

Within minutes after leaving the park I was struggling to maintain momentum. We were barely out of the gate on the final 65-mile leg of the Ride with Larry and I was sucking wind. They simply don't make hills like this in Florida – and it wasn't just one hill, it leveled off for a moment and then the angle steepened. The training I'd undertaken back home didn't prepare me for a hill of this size, especially without any advance warm-up.

So, I did one of the last things that I wanted to do – I put my foot down, dismounted, and pushed my bike the last 30 yards to the top of the hill. At that point, I remounted, caught my breath, turned to my son, Brian, who was riding along with me and said, "Let's ride."

Very motivational, until I glanced up and realized that we had one more hill to conquer before the road flattened out. An image flashed through my mind of a T-shirt that I'd seen a month before during the Mayor's Ride to Work Day in Orlando. It read, "DLF > DNF > DNS – Dead Last Finish is greater than Did Not Finish, which greatly trumps Did Not Start." I might have paused for a moment, but I was committed to seeing this through. It was going to be a loooooooooong day! This was quickly turning into one heck of an adventure.

The road did level off and Brian and I got into a pedaling rhythm. Brian was riding a sleek Bianchi Iseo, which he noted several times through-out the day as being "much nicer" than his bike at home. Despite several warnings from cycling friends, I had rented a 21-speed Electra Townie because that's what I ride at home and it's easier on my back and shoulders. I know the limitations for climbing due to the bike's weight and unique "flat foot technology" design, but I figured it was better to go with the beast that I knew than try to undertake this journey on something that I hadn't ridden.

The goal for the day was to ride from Sioux Falls through Beresford (about 35 miles) and continue to Vermillion (another 30 miles). Larry and Betty Smith live in Vermillion and a celebration was planned for 1:00 p.m. sharp. Everyone later agreed – even for most of the experienced cyclists – six hours to cover 65 miles was aggressive. For a 59-year-old, pleasingly plump rider on a less-than-ideal machine, it was going to be a challenge. That led to my decision to humbly take advantage of a few SAG rides. SAG stands for "support and gear" vehicles that follow the cyclists and are available to change bike tires, make minor repairs, or give rides to slow or fatigued riders. I later named the drivers of our support vehicles my "angels of mercy." I had broadcasted to the world that I was undertaking a 65-mile bike ride – a number that is impressive, in fact it qualifies as a "metric century" since 62 miles equals 100 kilometers. After having

completed 45 miles on the West Orange Trail in 95-degree temperatures, I thought this would be a piece of cake with the cooler
weather. Due to the time constraint and certainly wanting to
take part in the final push into Vermillion, I accepted the SAG's
hospitality. In fact, the rides gave me an opportunity to get to
know Leland Smith (Larry and Betty's son) and his girlfriend,
Sarah – both of whom do great work with nonprofits in Wash-
ington, D.C; as well as Emi from Hawaii – also known as the
"fifth" Theiss sister (Betty's family), who is President of a nonprofit health support group. Betty even rode along with us at one
point. She's a strong cyclist but as the primary organizer of this
event, she had to stay ahead of the pack. I had a very meaningful
conversation with her about Larry's DBS (deep brain stimulation
surgery) – part of my networking effort to catalogue PD information that I might need one day.

For anyone now reading this who may be disappointed to find
out that I didn't have my "Cinderella day" and remain in contact
with the pedals for the full 65 miles, I extend an apology – but
the sum-total experience of the day made up for it. I "officially"
logged 34.68 of the toughest miles that I've ever ridden. There
were several more serious hills to climb throughout the day,
which I scaled without ever setting my foot down again. The 8
– 10 mph breeze at the beginning of the day ramped up to 18 –
20 mph as we clawed our way into Vermillion along Highway
19. I felt very pleased with my accomplishment for the day. I
know that I could have ridden more with additional physical
training, a more appropriate bike and sufficient time to complete the route. However, putting my preparation into perspective, I did log 150 miles in June in high Florida heat prior to
traveling to South Dakota. Just not enough time spent training
on hills. But just like dealing with PD, you simply have to play
the cards that you are dealt. It was good to learn that day that
it's perfectly acceptable to ask for – and graciously accept – help
from time to time.

A highlight of the day was when we met up with the lead group about five miles outside Beresford. Many of the riders had stopped for a rest break. When they started back up, Caroline (one of Betty's sisters) called for me to ride in the front next to Larry. We had a blast, just chatting away and joking. He's a really funny guy. After our "private moment" – difficult to have privacy with the documentary film crew driving ahead of us with the camera and microphone capturing our every word – we were joined by some of the other Parkinson's patients. One of those riding a trike was a gentleman named Wendall, who was 95 years old at the time! He rode the entire route with a bit of an assist from one of his supporters who hooked up a rope to help him get up some of the hills by gently pulling him while Wendall continued to pedal. Shortly after that moment, one of the guys called back, "Bring up the Catrikes" and all of the three-wheeled speed demons raced to the front. They still had 40 miles to go and these guys were playing "dodge 'em" with these nimble little vehicles. (Professor Steve from the University of South Dakota told me later that he's been clocked at 55 mph on his Catrike). When they all moved forward like an attack squadron, I drifted back and swore that I could hear musical strains of "Flight of the Valkyries" playing across the South Dakota plains.

The group stopped briefly in Beresford and additional riders joined us. In total, there were over 150 cyclists. We picked up

87

more hills south of town but I was mentally and physically prepared by that time. Brian and I went screaming down one hill and I glanced at my bike computer displaying 22 mph at the bottom – a new record for me. We virtually glided up the ensuing climb on the other side. We passed Betty on the way down the hill and thought it was great that she'd stopped to cheer people on – turns out that she had a flat tire, but since she'd already 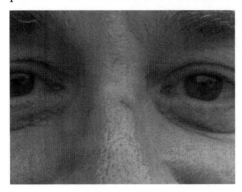 called for a replacement bike, she didn't want anyone stopping to help her so she played cheerleader instead.

After that climb we crossed over a road and Brian realized that we'd missed a turn and asked me to stop. I obliged and pressed on my brakes – forgetting one important thing – I was clipped in to my pedals. I frantically tried to unclip, but started to sense that I was falling. I had only begun using clipless pedals a few weeks before, and had been warned by many people that "you will fall over." I'd previously thought that wasn't an option. But now it was happening to me. I simply decided – rather quickly – to just "go with it" and completely relaxed. I twisted enough that I "executed" a perfect stunt fall – landing first on my butt, then my back and finally my helmet tapped the ground but protected my head. I realized that I'd scraped my left calf – providing me with bragging rights to some South Dakota "road rash" as a souvenir. Otherwise, I felt fine. I was rather amused by the whole situation. Not so for poor Brian, who had to helplessly watch this take place right before his eyes. He was naturally concerned, but I informed him that I was perfectly fine, wasn't seeing stars and was ready to continue. He said, "But your whole head is bleeding." He recalls that my face was covered with blood. In actuality, the bridge of my nose had sustained a cut from my sunglasses. I was able to control the bleeding and we resumed our ride.

Back on the right road, we enjoyed about half an hour of virtually no wind, no cars, a fresh stretch of asphalt, and a slight downhill grade – pedaling effortlessly at a steady 18 mph.

Then came Highway 19, a major two-lane thoroughfare. For my Cycling Savvy friends, this wasn't a road where one "controlled the lane." Doing so would have almost immediately been met with eighteen wheels rolling up your back. The traffic was screaming on that road 70+ mph. We had a 6 – 8-foot section to ride in, but the strong headwinds combined with the wind gusts from passing vehicles made this a very slow, arduous portion of the journey. To add insult to injury, there was one more hill to conquer as we approached Vermillion. The slow grade down to it was pleasant, despite what I nicknamed the "mine field" – lots of rocks and pebbles in our lane due to spring rain runoff. In the process of steering around the rocks, I had come to a full stop at the bottom, so had to start the climb with no momentum. I worked my gears down to the second to the lowest – the first had me simply spinning and didn't do any good. I ended up naming that second gear the "Little Engine That Could" gear – because with every pedal stroke I was telling myself, "I think I can, I think I can." It was slow, it was gritty, but I made it! Just after reaching the plateau, we saw Emi parked to the side of the road with her SAG truck. Her one question was, "would you like a peanut bar?" While I did manage my hydration and nutrition fairly well throughout the day, my "fuel tank" was plumb empty at that point. I think the first bite was half wrapper and half bar. It tasted great!

 We knew we were getting close, and after crossing a major highway, saw many of the riders assembled in a parking lot. As we rode in, a cheer went up from the group, signifying that we'd "done good." It was such an honor to be meeting up with the others and riding in with my son by my side. Sure, we took a couple of SAG rides, but we had accomplished so much together that day. For one thing, I had said, "In YOUR FACE, Parkinson's!" by pursuing and accomplishing my goal of completing the ride. The organizers had held Larry back so he could ride in with a police escort. The group reassembled and prepared for the final trek into Vermillion.

The whole town must have come out. Entire families lined the roadway with signs and flags. As we passed one sign that said, "Only 1 more mile to go" a combined sigh of relief and a groan went out from the riders. Just fifty feet later, however, another lady had a sign that said, "Only 2 more miles to go" – nice one! The group turned down Main Street and hundreds more people were assembled to greet us. A live band was playing, food stands were set up, and a crowd was waiting for Larry's victorious return after his 300-mile adventure. One of his good friends handed him a beer as he took to the stage and enjoyed the well-deserved adulation of all gathered. People talk about Ironman competitions, but what Larry accomplished was simply mind-boggling and incredibly inspirational. I will not forget the joy on his face anytime soon.

I was so very proud of my son, Brian. He watched over me like a hawk all day long. When we decided to do this ride together, he didn't even own a bike, but got one a month out and found time to fit in a reasonable amount of advance training time out in California. He encouraged me every step of the way. I'm very sorry that I scared him when I fell, but I was emboldened to accomplish my ride by his love and support. In addition, I could strongly sense the virtual good wishes coming my way from my wife, Laura; our daughter, Jen, and her husband, Bob. Thank you to Brian's wife, Jessica, who shared him for several days to participate in my dream. A giant "group hug" to Larry, Betty, their families and all the other wonderful people I met as part of this experience.

The celebration in downtown Vermillion after Larry and his entourage crossed the finish line was a genuine slice of Americana. Larry's neighbors and friends truly love and admire him. When the after-party was wrapping up, Brian and I boarded a van for the return to Sioux Falls. Someone tossed us two loaves of bread from Larry's bakery. Back in our room we celebrated the day with the bread, some salami and cheese, and uncorked a bottle of Conn Creek Anthology wine. The perfect end to a perfect day. The bread, by the way, was everything that I'd heard it would be!

Relaxing back in our hotel room, I decided to check my fundraising webpage. Due to the generosity of friends and family, I had increased my goal several times leading up to the ride. I had raised about $3,700 before the ride, mostly in small donations of $5, $10, and $20. I'd been hoping to raise $4,000 and was astounded when I opened the donation page and saw that the total was over $4,000, with one donation of $300. Receiving $50 or even $100 from supporters is generous, so $300 is significant. I wondered who might have been so generous and immediately thought of one friend for whom the ride held a great deal of significance. Her name is Amanda Hite, a social media wizard. When I told her a month or so earlier that I would be raising money for Parkinson's disease, she stopped me and shared that her grandfather had Parkinson's and that he was the most important person in the world to her. The next day she tweeted out my donation page to her 30,000 followers. I wrote to her that evening and asked if she might know who placed the mystery donation. She immediately knew that it was a friend of hers named Scott. They were speaking while I was on the ride and he told her, "Your friend is out on the road today, let's put his goal over the top right now." So, the donation that caused me to hit my target came from someone I didn't even know, but who did so to support his friend and her grandfather. That prompted me to later create a virtual event called the "Grandparents Ride." It was to celebrate grandchildren who admire grandparents who are living well with Parkinson's and grandparents who wish to demonstrate to their grandchildren that they are not giving up, despite dealing with this condition.

After taking part in this ride, I firmly believe in the Davis Phinney Foundation's motto – "Every Victory Counts." I experienced a string of many progressive victories throughout the day. After getting off my bike on 57th Street, when all the other riders were out of sight, I could have just rolled back down to the parking lot. But with Brian by my side, I got back on my bike and kept moving. It's all about perseverance, one pedal stroke after another. This was the most exhilarating ride of my life, but far from my last. I may travel at "Bike Speed," but look for me out there riding around with a smile on my face.

PD Heroes – POPS Ride – Phoenix, AZ

The first POPs Ride took place in 2011. Brothers Shane and Shannon Stutzman rode their bicycles from St. Augustine, FL to San Diego, CA, a distance of about 3,100 miles. The reason for their ride was to honor their father, Jerry Stutzman, who lives with Parkinson's. "POPs" is an acronym for "Pedaling Over Parkinson's" and an endearment for their dad. When describing why they rode from East to West, the two shared that their dad fights an uphill battle with PD every day. The least that they could do is to ride uphill and into the wind.

Shane and Shannon's passion is to help everyone they meet to understand a little more about Parkinson's, its impact on lives, and current treatments. They believe in the expression, "knowledge is power." Their goal is to connect those who need the knowledge with those who have the knowledge.

Their ride was successful and their father, Jerry, even joined them for part of the event when they passed through their home state of Arizona. Their arrival in San Diego was a joyous moment with many family members and friends there to greet them.

In 2014, the brothers once again took to the road. This time the route was along the Pacific Coast Highway, from Vancouver, B.C. to San Diego, CA. They rode from April 28th to May 5th. Accompanying them were their father, Jerry, and Parkinson's legend, Carl Ames. I followed that ride with great interest, cheering them from afar. Their motto for the PCH Ride was "Parkinson's Can't Hold 'Em."

Shane and Shannon have continued with their volunteer efforts and their work in spreading knowledge to the Parkinson's Community. They have helped out at Davis Phinney Foundation Victory Summits, from Las Vegas all the way to the country of Malaysia. They even lent their encouragement and support to help me on my quest of taking part in the Las Vegas Parkinson's Unity Ride.

Young men like Shane and Shannon are a blessing to not only their own father, but to the many in the PD Community with whom they come in contact. Pedal on, boys!

CHAPTER 11

Central Park in Fall

WHILE BUSINESS TRAVEL OFFERS the opportunity to visit many wonderful cities, that often simply means flying in, taking a taxi to a hotel, and "touring" the inside of another all-too-familiar lobby and set of meeting rooms. Then it's a quick dash back to the airport and jetting off to the next destination.

The spirit and philosophy of "Bike Speed" is to make a conscious effort to carve out time for yourself to actually participate in the environment where your travel takes you. Your company paid for you to attend the event and expects you to devote your efforts to meeting with clients and learning from presentations. The conference agenda may be jam-packed. However, with a bit of advance planning or flexibility, it is possible to make the trip much more meaningful. You can get your work done and still find time to enjoy the hidden gems in the surrounding area.

From October 8-10, 2011, I was in New York City to attend a customer's annual convention. Their theme was "Taking the Stage" and the backdrop for the general sessions resembled a look down Times Square and marquees from all the famous plays. Broadway performers provided a break between speakers and they had marvelous voices. One entertainer had performed the role of Mustafa in the Lion King over 3,000 times – he sang the song *Impossible Dream* from the Man of La Mancha and gave everyone in the audience goose bumps. Another evening, entertainment after dinner was provided by Gary Sinise and the Lieutenant Dan Band (yup, the same person who played Lt. Dan in Forrest Gump and went on to star in CSI – New York.) The band performs about 50-75 shows per year, including shows for military troops around the world and at home. They covered a wide range of songs and were a lot of fun to see in person.

When I checked into the hotel, I saw a sign for bike rentals. I was staying at the New York Hilton, which is only a few blocks south of Central Park. I gathered some information and made plans to return the following day. Unfortunately, when I went back about 4:00 p.m. on Sunday, the counter was closed for the day. I grabbed my iPad and quickly Googled bike rentals in the area and found the Central Park Bicycle Shop, which was just five blocks away. I quickly made a reservation and earned a discount for booking online – paying just $8.00 for a one-hour rental. The shop was two blocks south of Central Park. I should have taken more time selecting the bike, since it wasn't the greatest ride. I've experienced that problem in the past, so I should create a "checklist" to guarantee a better experience. Sure wish I could use my own bike when I travel. I may have to invest in a folding travel bike one day!

I started off by heading east on 57th Street, then turning north on 8th Avenue. That took me to Columbus Circle (built in 1905), a major New York City landmark. I used the techniques learned in my Cycling Savvy class and easily navigated this four-lane roundabout. Traffic was reasonably light since it was a Sunday afternoon. But nonetheless, it was still Columbus Circle – that was crazy exciting! Here's a view that I snagged from Wikipedia of a photo taken of the Circle from within the Time Warner Building. For those who watch "Anderson" (Anderson Cooper's daytime show), his set looks out on this same view.

I then proceeded north up Central Park West in the bike lane with taxis whizzing by on my left. I entered Central Park at 67th Street. If I'd done a bit more advance research, I would have gone on to the 72nd Street entrance instead, which leads directly to "Strawberry Fields," the garden containing the Imagine mosaic honoring John Lennon – after all, the day of my ride was October 9th, John Lennon's birthday.

I joined the parade of horse drawn carriages, cyclists, roller bladers, and pedestrians on the one-way loop around the park. While it was "organized chaos," everyone was in a great mood due to the perfect Indian summer day – not a cloud in the sky, temperature in the high 70s. With my interest in stopping here and there to take pictures, I was probably crisscrossing traffic more than most. Every level of rider was represented, from true novices, to families cruising along together, to serious cyclists. It was a fantastic and eclectic gathering. The picnic areas and public lawns were full of people sitting on blankets and simply enjoying each other's company. The mood and merriment evident throughout the park's 843 acres that day must have been exactly what the designers had in mind when they first opened it back in 1857.

Rolling along Center Drive, I passed the Carousel. The original carousel burned in a fire, but was replaced by the current one in 1950 – a year before I was even born – now that's old! I maneuvered my way to the side of the road and took a photo.

I made a stop at the Loeb Boathouse, a popular spot for lunch and renting boats. While I was reviewing the menu, I looked up the lane and an entire wedding party was making their way around the boathouse to pose for photos. In spite of all the people in the park that day, I'm sure that their photographer was able to capture some beautiful images, since the park looked fantastic and the lighting was perfect. Off in the distance were the twin towers of the San Remo Building, a 27-story luxury apartment. The names of some of its past and present residents are rather familiar – Stephen Sondheim, Donna Karan, Stephen Spielberg, Steve Jobs, Demi Moore, Glenn Close, Dustin Hoffman, Bono, Steve Martin, Eddie Cantor, Hedy Lamarr, and Rita Hayworth. Nice neighborhood.

While I didn't have time to stay for dinner, the menu at the Loeb Boathouse was rather enticing.

I pressed on and passed the Jacqueline Kennedy Onassis Reservoir and turned west above the North Meadow, rejoining the West Drive headed south. Even though it was approaching dusk, plenty of people were still enjoying their ride on rented boats or strolling along the water's edge. Over the course of a single hour, the light had changed the atmosphere from midday to the promise of a romantic evening.

It was getting close to the time to return my rented bike, so I exited the magic of Central Park onto 7th Avenue. I rode two blocks and turned right back onto 57th Street, crossed Broadway and cruised up to the Central Park Bike Shop. I was right on time. Even though I'd only been out for an hour, I'd taken in so much in that short period of time.

New York City's motto is "I Love New York." I was fortunate to snap this photo from my hotel room on the 27th floor looking down onto the Avenue of the Americas and catch this statue framed in a sunbeam. It perfectly captured my feeling about this trip and the wonderful city that I had the privilege of visiting.

On my next trip I might spend a bit more time planning the area where I will be riding to make sure that I don't miss anything. I will also be more selective about the bike that I choose for my journey – and welcome any suggestions from my readers on how to do just that. But most of all, I am so very glad that I took one hour out of an active business trip to see Central Park – at Bike Speed. I hope that you get to do the same one day.

PD Heroes – PWR Class – Altamonte Springs, FL

In 2010. Becky Farley created a special fitness center in Tucson, AZ, focused on people with Parkinson's. She translated cutting-edge research on exercise and brain change into real-world healthcare and wellness programs for PD patients. The program is called "Parkinson's Wellness Recovery" or PWR! for short. The group also offers PWR! Retreats, a week-long program for People with Parkinson's and their Care Partners, focused on exercise, education, enrichment, and empowerment.

Fortunately, for those who do not live near Tucson or are unable to attend the PWR! Retreat, instructors are being trained to deliver classes around the country. In my area, Florida Hospital in the Orlando area adopted the program in 2015. PWR! Instructor Dr. Claire McClean trained several exercise physiologists and physical therapists to lead classes.

I describe the classes as a combination of stretching, yoga and tai chi. The flexibility helps people with Parkinson's, regardless of where they are with the disease. Classes are offered at five locations in our area three times per week. The basic movements are easily learned and can be done in class, at home, or even when traveling. I've found this to be a great benefit for flexibility.

An interesting phenomenon has occurred since I began the class. There are all levels of participants in our group, which averages about 12 per class. Several of us still have fairly good balance and flexibility, a few require walkers, and one or two are cognitively challenged. Our trainer, Andrea Molina, is very patient and kind with those who take more time to process instructions. That has taught the rest of us to have patience as well. This is not a contest, we are all simply trying to do our best and to support each other. If I miss class for a while, the others are sincerely interested in my wellbeing and how I'm doing. The connection that we have made with each other reminds me of the Dance for PD classes, which Dave Iverson described in his film *Capturing Grace*.

CHAPTER 12

1,000 Mile Goal

AFTER MY TRIP TO SOUTH DAKOTA for the Ride With Larry event, I had pedaled about 550 miles. Even though I had slacked off a bit in July and August due to the Florida heat and humidity, I continued to amass more miles. With the one-year anniversary of my Cycling Savvy class on November 13th, I decided to go for 1,000 miles.

With two weeks remaining, I was up to 875 miles and just had 125 miles to go. I was closing in on that goal. It was doable, but would require dedication. During a First Friday Ride, I mentioned my plan to Charles Badger, the ultra-distance rider I had met earlier in the year. He offered to help me reach my goal by joining me on two rides during the remaining couple of weeks.

Boys and Girls Club Ride

Charles had previously agreed to accompany a group of riders for a ride to benefit the Boys and Girls Clubs in our area. We met at the AAA headquarters on Sunday, November 6th. Charles reviewed the route with me and asked me to take the lead. He would follow behind the group and "shepherd our flock." Being asked to "lead the dance" was a big honor and even a larger responsibility. The phrase was coined by Keri Caffrey, Founder of Cycling Savvy, and is best understood as a way to ride with confidence.

Our group of 25 riders consisted of representatives from a finance company, their clients, family and friends. I noticed that two of the ladies were riding bikes like mine. When I asked them about their bikes and asked if they rode very often, they acknowledged that they hadn't taken them out of the garage in more than a year. This was going to be a long day for them, but they did well throughout the ride.

We started along International Parkway. I quickly discovered that a disadvantage of "riding point" (in front) was contending with headwinds and carving a path through the wind for the rest of the riders. We seemed to be riding directly into the wind much of the day. However, we had a pleasant tailwind as we rode along the south side of Lake Monroe. We made our way through the town of Sanford. It was a beautiful day.

Much of our 30-mile ride was along country roads and everyone appreciated the scenery and the opportunity to converse with one another. As we rode near a pasture of horses, I started a mini stampede when I rang my bike bell. The ponies settled down in their corral as we rolled past them. Since the roads were virtually free of cars, the ride was a relaxing way to spend time together and support a good cause.

During the midpoint rest stop, I saw Michael Cottle. He and his wife, Arden, are the owners of OutSpoken Bikes in Lake Mary – the shop where I had purchased my bike. He was surprised to see me leading the group on my Townie. Many cycling friends have recommended that I move up to a road bike, but the current transportation has been a great ride and served me well for many miles. I love my bike!

At the last stop, Charles asked me to explain the chalk drawings that he had made on the pavement describing how to handle the remaining interchanges. It was gratifying to share my cycling knowledge with the group. I also thanked them for helping me move closer to my goal of riding 1,000 miles and shared the fact that I had Parkinson's disease, explaining the benefits of cycling as therapy for Parkinson's patients.

After navigating Country Club Road, Lake Mary Blvd. and Reinhardt Road sections, we finally approached the bridge over I-4. Charles rode up next to me and I admitted, "I got nothing left for the bridge." My mentor immediately shot back some words of encouragement, which was just what I needed. I executed the first turn onto the ramp by going down to my second gear, but the 180-degree turn was too much, so I dismounted and let the group pass. I admit to walking my bike up to the apex of the bridge, but sailed off the downside ramp at about 20 mph and rejoined the group at the point where they had gathered and was met with a round of applause from "my peeps." I resumed my spot up front and brought the herd back to the starting point.

We were each given a medal upon our return. Later I realized that it read "Century Ride," recognition for completing the 100-mile route. Our group had only completed about 40 miles, and while I'm all for being honest, I rationalized that I would soon be reaching my goal of the equivalent of "Ten Centuries," so I proudly placed the medal around my neck.

Veteran's Day Ride – Final Push to my Goal

Charles showed up Friday morning at our meeting spot behind the Peach Valley Cafe. He was accompanied by a co-worker, Ryan Warner, who was wearing a U.S. Marine Corps logo on his jersey. It was very fitting to be doing this ride on Veteran's Day (11/11/11) with a veteran. Ryan, thank you for your service to our country!

I only needed 18.42 miles to reach the goal. Charles had mapped out a 35-mile route. We again passed the AAA building as we rode up International Parkway. However, we quickly encountered 16-mph headwinds, which slowed our progress. When we reached Highway 17-92, we crossed the Old St. John's River Bridge. Halfway up the ascent I elected to walk my bike to avoid pulling a muscle. Charles and Ryan waited patiently at the top. We took a moment to catch our breath and pose for a few photos with the I-4 Bridge in the background.

We turned onto the Spring to Spring Trail. It winds through a tree-lined path, providing protection from the wind. Ryan saw a wild pig and Charles pointed out several deer in one meadow. Along the way, we took in views of Lake Monroe with the mid-morning sunlight dancing off the waves.

We left the trail at Dirksen Drive. After a mile on that busy road, we turned onto Main St. through the town of Enterprise, a perfect example of old Florida, with restored buildings dating back to the late 1800's. Next, we turned left onto Enterprise Osteen Road. It offered several miles of live oak trees, dripping with Spanish moss, which provided a lush canopy of greenery. We were rapidly approaching the goal.

I began calling out the countdown as we completed each remaining mile. My companions allowed me to ride alone up front to savor the moment. Five, four, three, two ….. With one mile to go, we passed a house with an American flag flying proudly in the wind. My countdown became "tenths" ….. and then we were there. Goal accomplished – 1,000 miles in one year!

Davis Phinney would celebrate every cycling victory by sitting up in the saddle and raising his arms into a "V" for victory. One of his Foundation's mottos is "Every Victory Counts." Achieving my goal was indeed a victory for which I am very proud. It was a pleasure to raise my arms up in celebration and to be photographed with my "Ride with Larry" shirt, which Davis Phinney had autographed for me at the Grand Rapids Victory Summit.

Reaching this personal goal didn't earn me a medal or have any significant meaning in the grand scheme of things. It did, however, prove to me that I can take on challenges and work steadily towards achieving them. I don't know how Parkinson's will affect me over time, but I am doing my best to fight back. The goal was personal, but achieving it was a "team victory" due in large part to the tremendous amount of support, encouragement, and love that I've received from family, friends, and complete strangers.

We resumed our ride and savored the beautiful fall day, smooth pavement, and the satisfaction that comes from "crossing the finish line." After winding around the east side of Lake Monroe, we headed west along Lake Mary Blvd., back towards our starting point. The final feature of the day was crossing the I-4 interchange on Lake Mary Blvd. It was a fitting way to complete our "Victory Lap." That interchange once was a major obstacle for me. I had navigated it for the first time two weeks after completing the Cycling Savvy class last year. Keri Caffrey coached me through it back them and her suggestions were still clear in my mind. These 1,000 miles were made up of many such small victories along the way. I plan to continue to cycle for as long as I can. Some of the future miles may be difficult, but they will all be a source of joy.

PD Heroes – The Ataxian, Kyle Bryant – Exxon, PA

Some of my heroes do not have Parkinson's disease. Through Mark Egeland, General Manager and Partner in Catrike, I learned about a condition called Friedreich's Ataxia. It is a debilitating, life-shortening, degenerative neuro-muscular disorder. Most individuals have onset of FA between the ages of 5 and 18. Seemingly perfectly healthy young people can contract this disease and lose the use of their muscles in a short time, requiring them to use wheelchairs to get around. This condition is treated by some of the same doctors who treat Parkinson's patients, so it is sort of a "cousin" disease. I've met some genuine heroes in the FA Community over the past few years.

Kyle was diagnosed with Friedreich's Ataxia at age 17. Previously he had lettered in several sports. Not to be held back, in 2007 he founded Ride ATAXIA with a 2,500 mile, 59-day ride from San Diego, CA to Memphis, TN to the National Ataxia Foundation annual membership meeting. That has since blossomed into six cycling events per year and has raised over $3 million for FA research.

He also participated in the Race Across America (RAAM) as part of 4-man Team FARA. The team completed the 3,000-mile non-stop race from San Diego, CA to Annapolis, MD in 8 days, 8 hours, and 14 minutes.

In 2015, during the Bob Cook Memorial Mt. Evans Hill Climb, Kyle rode his Catrike to the highest paved road in America at Mt. Evans in Colorado, an elevation of 14,000'.

Kyle stars in the documentary film The Ataxian, which chronicles his personal journey of becoming the national FA spokesman.

In addition to being an FA Warrior, fundraising Wizard, and cycling expert, Kyle is also one of the nicest guys you could ever meet. Ride Ataxia events can be found at www.curefa.org. I've had the privilege of taking part in several of the ones in Orlando.

CHAPTER 13

Climbing a Mountain in Scotland

WHILE BIKING HAS BEEN MY FAVORITE form of exercise for some time, I thought that I would add some variety to my routine. Some might call that "cross training," but I decided to set a "stretch goal" and have a go at mountain climbing.

A few years ago, I met Roger Barr from Airdrie, Scotland. He hikes for fun, but just a bit farther than most people. One of Roger's hobbies is "Munro Bagging." A "Munro" is a mountain in Scotland with a height of over 3,000 ft. There are 283 such mountains in Scotland. Several years ago, Roger set out to climb all of them, an accomplishment shared by a rather small group of people. He recorded his first Munro in 1994 by ascending Aonach Eagach Ridge, the most dangerous ridge walk in Scotland. He achieved his goal in 2006 by reaching the peak of Ladhar Bheinn. In addition, he takes "wee walks," which often consist of several hundred miles at one time. He completed the Coast to Coast Walk covering 192 miles and spanning the width of Great Britain. He also hiked from the most southern point in

England to the most northern spot in Scotland over the course of several walks. To say the least, Roger knows a bit about hillwalking.

At one point, I asked Roger to take me up a Munro. He agreed, but we had yet to set the time and place. When I found that I would be taking a business trip to London in February, 2012, I saw it as the opportunity to take that hike. After wrapping up the meetings, I took the train from London to Glasgow and spent the weekend with Roger and his wife, Margaret. One of the items on our itinerary was a hike in the Trossachs and a climb up Ben A'an. While this "mini-mountain" stands 1,491 ft. in height and doesn't officially qualify as a Munro, this was my best chance at fulfilling my dream of doing some serious hillwalking with Roger.

The day before striking out for Ben A'an, Roger and I visited the ruins of Bothwell Castle, which is located on the River Clyde in South Lanarkshire. While it was an enjoyable tour, I'm convinced Roger used the short walk around the castle as a way to test my hiking ability. Apparently I passed the test, since we loaded up our gear and headed out to Ben A'an on Sunday morning. In less than an hour we arrived at the car park. Roger had expected only a handful of vehicles, but a break in the weather brought quite a few other hikers out to enjoy the day. We laced up our hiking boots, donned a few layers of jumpers (meaning "sweaters," for non-Scottish folks), stowed away some snacks, and were on our way. Roger's wife, Margaret, joined us.

Immediately after passing the entry sign, the trail became steep. The first section consists of packed dirt with exposed tree roots crisscrossing the path. Margaret charged ahead at her own pace, but Roger followed me and provided a steady stream of encouragement. Several times he told me, "This is not a race, go at your own pace," or "If you get tired, feel free to stop," or "Watch your feet, choose the best route for you." Between the excitement of actually being on this hike and getting used to the activity, I quickly began to perspire and question whether I was capable of this adventure. But I pressed on. As I've mentioned in relation to cycling, I dropped down into my "Little Engine That Could" gear and fully committed to making it to the summit – even on my hands and knees if that's what it took.

Stopping every once in a while to take pictures was a pleasant relief from the focus required to execute the climb safely. I was very glad that I had borrowed a pair of hiking sticks from Roger. They helped me maintain my balance and provided necessary support in some tricky sections.

A bridge across the stream was a point of reference that we'd made it one third of the way. Naturally it provided a photo opportunity, as well as a way to catch my breath and pause to appreciate the beauty all around. It also was an indication that the trail was about to get steeper. Just past the bridge we were treated to a view of Loch Achray.

Every once in a while, the mountain offered some forgiveness and flattened out for a bit. In one section, we waited for some hikers who were descending. A woman in the group had slipped while crossing a particularly muddy section of the bog, and was covered in "gunk." We waited until they were out of earshot before sharing an impolite chuckle about her plight.

Soon after we were afforded our first view of the Ben A'an summit through the trees, a view that would be impossible during the summer when full foliage was in place. We paused at the base of the summit to take photos and enjoy a nibble of trail mix and other snacks. At this point, Roger informed me that we were already two-thirds of the way to the summit. I was feeling strong and knew that I'd already accomplished a great deal in reaching this point. Some of my friends, perhaps even Roger, had doubts about my ability to navigate this climb, but I was determined to see it through. After all, the best view is from the top, so we pressed forward.

The summit still looked like a long way off, but we were prepared for the challenge. The biggest difference was the fact that the boulders were larger and the height of each stepping stone was noticeably higher than the lower sections back in the woods. Some people call Ben A'an the "giant staircase." I was about to find out just what they meant.

My focus was on placing my feet carefully to avoid toppling over backwards. For the most part, we were above the snow, but began to find ice along the way as we approached the top of the mountain. In spite of being cautious and watching for ice, I felt my pace quicken the closer that we got to the top. I was actually going to do this! I was literally being pushed along by an adrenaline rush. We were now within 10 feet of the summit, but the last stretch was solid ice. Roger planted his foot sideways for me to use as an anchor, but the slippery slope prevented me from making any progress. We looked around and chose to scramble across a patch of heather in order to reach the summit. As I'd predicted earlier, I was bound and determined to complete this hike – even on my hands and knees – which proved to be necessary.

To say that the view was spectacular would be an understatement. It was utterly peaceful. Even though there were at least a dozen people at the top, everyone treated this area like a shrine – not a word was spoken, everyone was taking in the splendor before them. The brief looks we exchanged with others spoke volumes of the shared experience. We had each done something very special that day. While this hike wasn't the most arduous considering the many other mountains in Scotland and peaks much higher in the Rockies and Sierra Nevada Range, I had accomplished a major goal on this day with my best friend. That made me very happy.

It began to get very cold at the top. While I would have enjoyed more time on the summit, Roger urged me to begin making our way back down. Of course, there was only one way to go, down the same way we climbed up.

I quickly discovered that walking down on a mountain was much more strenuous than walking up. It simply puts a lot more pressure on your quads. Roger told me that my bike riding probably helped me a great deal on this hike, but the return was a challenge. We were quickly passed by others.

As we returned to the forest, we approached that bog that had caused the lady to slip. I was commenting on the fact that while it was a muddy area, there were sturdy stones all along the way. Except for that next step – the one where my right leg sunk in to the muck above my knee. No problem, right? Simply lift my leg out and go on. Except that I couldn't move my leg and any attempt seemed to be pulling me in deeper like quicksand. Roger came to my rescue and was able to extract me from the bog without dislocating my shoulder. This scene caused Margaret to howl with laughter. Kind of funny, unless you're the one stuck in the mud! We did all share quite a chuckle about that for the rest of the hike.

This day was a great adventure. While I hope to climb Ben A'an again one day, or tackle some other mountains, my first scramble to the top will be a vivid memory for the rest of my life.

Roger Barr and John Alexander

We certainly didn't set any speed records that day. I later learned that the actual distance from the car park to the summit is 1.25 miles, so we hiked approximately 2.5 miles. However, when you add in nearly 1,400 feet of vertical gain and that much again in the descent, it was a rather respectable trek. I may have been the last one off the mountain that day, but I left it with a sense of pride and satisfaction. I am honored to have completed something that few get a chance to even attempt. Not bad for a 60-year-old with Parkinson's disease. The phrase goes "every victory counts," and this one meant a great deal to me.

Video Bonus– If you want to see a really crazy way that one cyclist conquered this mountain, go to YouTube and type in "Joe Barnes rides Ben A'an."

PD Heroes – Emily Penn Baudin – Dallas, TX

Emily Penn Baudin   Emily with Davis Phinney

When she was just 15 years old, Emily Penn was diagnosed with Friedreich's Ataxia. She had been diagnosed with scoliosis when she was a child, but remained active playing soccer, swimming, and running track. It wasn't until she noticed a twitch while running track that her family thought something else might be wrong. By the time she was 21, she was noticing more signs that her coordination was beginning to fade. Her handwriting was getting sloppier and she had begun to need a walker to get around.

Even though her condition was progressing, Emily continued to work out and train. She was given a Catrike by the Texas Irish Foundation and Richardson Bike Mart. She began training at the Dallas Cycle Center, a facility that trains every rider from novices to elite cyclists. Her recumbent bike is placed on a roller so she can ride in place, and is connected to a sophisticated computer that provides a myriad of detailed information about her ride. That helped prepare her for her first 25-mile outdoor bike ride. When that day came, it was cold, rainy, and windy. Emily was not able to complete the full distance that day due to the elements, but returned to the training center, doubled her training efforts, and achieved the 25-mile goal the next time she attempted that distance.

Emily has participated in several Ride Ataxia events and her smiling face provides hope to others with FA. Kyle Bryant said of Emily, "Over the last few years, Emily has become the absolute force in the fight against FA. We couldn't thank her enough for being an amazing person that other people with FA can look up to and take cues from the positive things that she is doing in her life."

When the Davis Phinney Foundation's Victory Summit came to Dallas, Mark Egeland set up a Catrike display to show the Parkinson's Community the benefit of riding a recumbent bike. He invited Emily to help out at the booth. Her enthusiasm was contagious and many people walked away inspired, including Davis Phinney himself.

Now age 23, Emily needs the use of a wheelchair to get around because her balance has declined. Nonetheless, she will be participating in the 2017 Ride Ataxia in Dallas. She met a wonderful young firefighter, Tye Baudin, through a Christian online dating service and they were married in 2016. With the support of her father and brother, she walked down the aisle. Emily delivered her healthy son, Logan, on May 31, 2017.

Of living with FA, Emily says, "People will say it's a setback, but it's a setup for something greater."

CHAPTER 14

Pedal On!

I WAS HOOKED ON CYCLING, and continued to find opportunities to take to the roads and trails. The First Friday rides provided a fun, social and relaxing opportunity to get together with friends, but I sought out more opportunities to challenge myself and achieve new goals.

Tour de Cure 2012

The Tour de Cure is a fundraiser for the Diabetes Association. While I don't have Diabetes, my brother does live with that condition. Riding in his honor made this 25-mile event all the more meaningful. I signed up as a single rider. This would be my longest distance by myself. The ride began at the University of Central Florida Medical School and looped around towards the Orlando International Airport. It was a well-organized ride, with groups doing various distances being released in waves. Starting with a large pack of riders was a bit hectic, but the first big hill allowed everyone to stretch out and settle into their own best pace. Having the first 1,000 miles under my belt, I felt comfortable on the ride and hung in there with various groups that I would connect with between rest stops. I felt good for the entire ride and was pleased to arrive back at the starting point ahead of several other riders.

On the drive home, I heard a strange noise from the back of my car. Looking in the rear-view mirror, I noticed that my bike was hanging off just one of the support arms on my bike carrier. Fortunately, I was able to stop safely and reposition the bike and double-check the tie-down straps. That was a close call. Though some might relish the excuse to buy a new bike, I was not yet ready to part with my Townie.

Copper Triangle 2012

Due to raising $5,000 during the Ride With Larry event the previous year, I received an invitation to attend the Davis Phinney Foundation's top fundraiser dinner in Colorado. That also included a ticket to ride in the "Copper Triangle" bike ride. The 78-mile course crests three Colorado mountain passes; Fremont Pass (elevation 11,318 feet), Tennessee Pass (elevation 10,424 feet), and Vail Pass (elevation 10,666 feet). The elevation gain is over 6,000 feet. Not only was that a longer distance than I had ever ridden, it was an insane amount of climbing compared to what I was accustomed to, living in Florida. One cycling friend commented that if I trained really hard, I might be able to handle the climbs; but I knew nothing about riding down mountain roads – I just might fly right off the mountain. To say the least, I heeded that advice. I declined the invitation to take part in the ride, however I did offer to serve as the group's photographer. That in itself was a lot of fun.

I got up at 5:00 a.m. to see the riders off on their adventure. Knowing that they would be on the course for several hours, Laura and I drove up to the Betty Ford Botanical Garden near Vail. As we were about to leave, the peloton of cyclists rolled past us on the last leg of the circuit. We made it back to Copper

Mountain in time to greet the riders and take photos of their triumphant return.

One of the riders completing the event was Carl Ames. I had met Carl and his wife, Leisa, at dinner the night before. Carl also lives with Parkinson's and had ridden the entire 78-mile Copper Triangle with his son, Jordan. We spoke for about twenty minutes and immediately became fast friends. After chatting for a bit, Carl suggested that we go over and talk with another person that he knew. However, he asked if he could lean on my arm since his PD medication was wearing off and he was experiencing a "freezing" episode, where his feet could barely shuffle along. This was after accomplishing a ride that the vast majority of "totally healthy" cyclists would never even attempt. It gave me insight into another one of the challenges that many people with Parkinson's face. It also demonstrated the depth of Carl's commitment to not let anything slow him down or prevent him from doing the activities that he loved.

Bike Falls Off Car – Not in the Plan

I was driving home on I-4 after a fun and enjoyable ride that ended at an ice cream parlor, I heard a noise, looked in the rearview mirror and realized that my bike had become detached from the bike rack, gone airborne, and smacked onto the roadway. I pulled over safely and parked in the emergency lane. I walked about 200 yards back to retrieve my bike and found it crumpled off to the side of the road. I'm sure that I heard a whimper as I approached.

I picked it up lovingly, acutely aware of the many scrapes and bruises it had incurred. The most obvious was that the front wheel was bent and the derailleur twisted, so it was impossible to roll it under its own power. I lifted it up and carried my Electra Townie back to my car. With a great degree of hesitancy, I placed it back in the cradle arms of the bike rack, which was still

123

firmly affixed to my car. Then I reattached the three rubber straps that were supposed to hold the bike securely in place, but had just failed – for the second time – resulting in the injuries my beloved bike had just sustained.

The rack is a Yakima King Joe 2, quite a sturdy device. I thought that I had checked and rechecked the straps after loading the bike on the car. In fact, the first time the bike dropped off the rack (driving home following the Tour de Cure ride earlier this year), I convinced myself that it must have been due to "operator error." I recalled placing the bike on the arms of the rack and going around the side to put my helmet and other items in the back seat. The possibility existed that I had not properly cinched down the straps properly. This time I had witnesses who saw me attach and double-check the tie-downs. A quick Google search of "strap failure" for this rack instantly presented at least ten instances of bikes separating from the King Joe while driving.

After contacting the manufacturer, I learned that due to the design of my Electra Townie's bike frame, I should have been using a "top bar" addition to keep the bike level. Without that, the rear wheel sits above the roof of the car and it is possible for a gust of wind, especially at highway speeds, to send the bike flying. It would have been nice to have known that before using the rack when I first bought it.

Among a number of parts of the bike that were damaged, crushed, or bent, the front fork was twisted. That was not easy to replace since the frame design had changed from the time I purchased my bike a few years earlier. I had a big ride scheduled for the following month and would have to use my son-in-law's bike as a substitute. The bike manufacturer did eventually replace my bike with a newer model.

Ride 4 Ronald – Metric Century – 2012

A "Metric Century" is a bike ride of 100 kilometers (62 miles). If I had ridden the full 65 miles during the Ride With Larry event, I would have been able to say that I had completed that cycling milestone. Instead I took a couple of SAG rides and my total was well below that distance. I don't regret taking advantage of the support, since that ensured that we would cross the finish line alongside Larry Smith and the rest of the group, plus I had some meaningful conversations while being shuttled further along the route.

When I saw that there was a fundraiser for the Ronald McDonald House and a metric century was one option, I jumped at the chance to take part in it. I'd been riding for almost two years and thought that I was finally prepared to take on this distance.

Two cycling friends agreed to accompany me on the ride. Larry Gies and Kathy LeBlanc are both very experienced riders familiar with the Orlando area. I knew that they would serve as guides and mentors to ensure that I would finish the distance and not get lost. We began the ride near Florida Hospital in downtown Orlando and headed west towards Winter Garden. Much of that route was along busy streets, but we rode along with the large pack of riders who had turned out for the event.

After a short break near Winter Park, we headed north towards Apopka, using the West Orange Trail. That was familiar to me since I'd ridden it a year before in preparation for the Ride With Larry. Another rest stop was set up in Apopka. We left that and headed west along a flat route to a subdivision called Errol Estates. We made a turn to enter the perimeter of the community and started down a steep hill. Naturally, after a fun ride down, we had to climb back up the other side. Larry Gies coached me on the specific points at which to shift gears and encouraged me throughout this section to keep pedaling. There are actually seven hills in that development. The going was slow at times, but I kept moving forward and was pleased to finish that section without stopping or putting my foot down.

When we returned to the Apopka rest area, Larry noticed that my face was very red. He told me to take off my bike helmet, fill a glass full of water from a cooler and pour it over my head. I did that about five times and began to feel better. The temperature was close to 100 degrees that day, so that rest stop probably saved me from heat exhaustion. While I was cooling down, Larry was talking with some friends who were completing the 100-mile route. He told me that one of the women had finished the Iron Man Triathlon in Hawaii a couple of times. I knew that she was one strong rider.

About five miles from the finish, my right foot became very painful. I had not switched out the standard rubber pedals on my son-in-law's bike with my clipless pedals, which meant that I was riding with regular tennis shoes instead of stiffer bike shoes. That caused an inflammation in my foot which was later diagnosed as Metatarsalgia. Just keeping my foot in contact with the pedal was excruciating and I had to stop every mile to take a break. Larry led the way and at times I wondered if Kathy was still with us, but she was shadowing me and staying close to my back tire. They patiently waited whenever I needed to take a break. I felt like a distressed fighter jet being guided back to the aircraft carrier by my wingmen.

We eventually made it back to Florida Hospital's parking lot and I was able to get off the bike and sit for a bit in a chair. While resting there, the woman Larry had been speaking with at the Apopka rest stop came up to me and congratulated me on "bagging my first metric century." I thought that was very kind of her, and it made me quite pleased with my accomplishment.

I would not have been able to finish that ride without the support and encouragement of Larry Gies and Kathy LeBlanc. I told them that they had been my "Guardian Angels" for the day, a term that I would use for many others who watched over me on rides in the future.

Next Milestone – 2,000 Miles Achieved at Sea

My wife, Laura, and I took a Royal Caribbean Cruise to the Western Caribbean in the fall of 2012. Renting a bike in port was an option, but I decided against that, since the traffic was often crazy and dangerous. Instead, I rode a stationary bike in the gym a few times and signed up for a couple of spin classes. One morning I took a spin class led by a young lady from Scotland. There were only two other people in the class – John Schier and his wife, Kathy, from Atlanta. They had ridden RAGBRAI (the ride across Iowa) the summer before and had plans for other long-distance rides together. The instructor took us along at a brisk pace, but that was all right, since we were able to stare out at the beautiful blue water as the ship glided along towards our next port of call. During that ride, I accumulated enough miles to reach my next cycling goal of 2,000 miles ridden since completing my Cycling Savvy class. I've always said that the class prepared me to ride "whenever and wherever I wanted." I never anticipated that some of those miles would be accomplished while cruising along at sea, but it sure made for a nice change of pace.

Inspiring Others to Ride

John and Monique

The accomplishment of riding my first 1,000 miles in 2011 caught the attention of a friend from my professional world. I had known Monique Donahue from CHART (Council of Hotel and Restaurant Trainers), since we both worked for companies that supported those industries. Monique asked if she could ride with me early in 2012. She had an old bike and struggled to keep up on the trail. Apparently, our conversation about consistently working towards a goal had made an impression upon her. I encouraged her to take the Cycling Savvy class and she signed up right away. In fact, she coined a phrase that they still use about cyclists belonging on the road: "I AM TRAFFIC." The next time I saw her, she had purchased a sleek new Orbea road bike and really trimmed down. Monique began to take part in many of the group rides and also

128

achieved her first metric century on the same day that I did. In fact, she tallied up her first 1,000 miles in about eight months, four less than it took me.

When I knew that I was about to reach my next milestone of 3,000 miles at the beginning of 2014, I asked Monique to join me on that ride of about fifteen miles. It was a perfect January day in Florida and we enjoyed simply riding along, chatting, and appreciating the camaraderie of having shared time together on our bikes.

I wanted to hit the 3,000-mile goal because I knew that I would be off my bike for a while. I was scheduled for a total shoulder replacement. This had nothing to do with Parkinson's, it was just wear and tear over a lifetime. Arthritis and bone spurs had built up in my right shoulder and were making it painful. That surgery turned out to be a good decision, but I was looking at five or six months of rehab before I could return to riding.

Parkinson's Unity Ride – Las Vegas 2015

My work frequently took me to Las Vegas to attend customer trade shows. I had a show on my calendar for February, 2015. Soon after I had committed to that event, I received a notice that the Davis Phinney Foundation would be hosting a Victory Summit in Vegas on Saturday of that same week. The Victory Summit® symposia deliver up-to-date information and practical tools that people with Parkinson's can use to live well today. Nationally recognized researchers, clinicians and physical therapists in the movement disorders field address the audience, which often numbers over 1,000 attendees. I had previously attended two other Victory Summits – one in Grand Rapids, Michigan and the other in Jacksonville, Florida. I decided to extend my week and go to the Las Vegas Victory Summit.

I received an invitation to take part in a Parkinson's Unity Ride. The timing couldn't have worked out better. The ride was being organized by Cidney Pratt Donahoo and her husband, Pat Donahoo. Cidney was diagnosed with Young Onset Parkinson's at age 47 and had been instrumental in building a support network for others in her situation in the Las Vegas area. Cidney and Pat are strong cyclists who have participated in RAGBRAI and Ride the Rockies. They had planned a day ride from a bike shop on the west side of Las Vegas up to Red Rock Canyon. I signed up right away.

I contacted the Las Vegas Cyclery bike shop to rent a bike. They suggested a mountain bike, since they didn't offer a hybrid like my Electra Townie. I thought that might work well, certainly better than a road bike for me.

After having shared my intention to take part in this ride on Facebook, I received a call from a college friend, Lisa Beth Heggeness, asking if she could join me for the ride. I agreed, and she made plans to travel from Reno with her husband, John, to be part of the event.

About a week before the ride, I received a note from Lauren Kehn. She is the Victory Crew Program Manager for the Davis Phinney Foundation. Lauren is an accomplished cyclist and has ridden the Copper Triangle event several times, including the year when I served as staff photographer. She told me that she would be my "riding buddy" for the day. That helped put my mind at ease because I knew that many of the riders would be very strong and probably far outpace me.

The morning of the Parkinson's Unity Ride arrived and I drove to the bike shop from my hotel. I had stopped by the afternoon before and gotten fitted for my bike, so I knew that it would be ready to go. I had brought along my own bike helmet and shoes, so I was ready to ride in no time. Others began to arrive and set up their bikes and gear. One guy walked over to me and introduced himself, simply saying, "Hi, I'm Jimmy." I learned his whole name later; Jimmy Choi. He had flown in from Chicago to take part. Another rider was Joe Williams, who had an entire "Go, Joe, Go" team with him. Then the most honored guests arrived – Davis Phinney, Olympic Bronze Medalist, and his wife, Connie Carpenter Phinney, Olympic Gold Medalist. Despite their past cycling accolades, they were simply here as another Parkie and Care Partner to ride in unity with a group of friends.

John and Lisa Beth

Lisa Beth and John flew down from Reno that morning and she was quickly set up with a bike to ride as well. While most of the riders were decked out in sleek cycling "kits," Lisa Beth comfortably wore jean shorts and a T-shirt. I wore bike shorts, but proudly had on my Ride with Larry T-shirt, which Davis had signed at the Grand Rapids Victory Summit. We fit right in, as no one was being judgmental that day.

After a greeting by Cidney and some advice for the ride, the group rolled out. The plan was for everyone to stay together until we began the climb on the other side of the freeway. Enthusiasm got the better of some of the folks and they were off like a shot. I settled into my position at the back of the pack, accompanied by Lauren and Lisa Beth. Two other riders joined us. They were the POPs Ride brothers, Shane and Shannon Stutzman. They told me that they were going to be the "sweepers" for the day and ride at the back of the pack. That meant that they would be riding with me.

The faster riders began pulling away as the grade up the hill became steeper. My four "Guardian Angels" hung back with me and we settled into our own pace. That pace, however, allowed us time to chat, take in the scenery, and appreciate the ride.

After climbing for several miles and just as we were about to make a turn to head towards Red Rock Canyon, we stopped for a brief rest. Polly Dawkins, Executive Director of the Davis Phinney Foundation, came up to me and suggested that it might be a good time for us to turn around. I was feeling fairly good at that point and began to mildly protest. She told me that the lead group was close to their final destination and would be coming back soon anyway and then she said, "You know that Lauren is pregnant and probably shouldn't be working so hard in this heat." I hadn't realized that Lauren was expecting, though I had been surprised to not see her the afternoon when I stopped by the convention center to help stuff bags for the Victory Summit attendees. Seems that someone had said she had the flu. Well, it obviously wasn't the flu that was impacting her.

Our group took Polly's advice and headed back down the hill. While the climb up the hill had been slow, it didn't seem that we'd gained much elevation, however going back down presented a different perspective. I wish that I'd had a bike computer on the rental because I know that I was flying downhill faster than I'd ever traveled on two wheels before. The only problem was that my hands were going numb. I could barely feel the brake levers. Nonetheless, thankfully we made it back safely to the Las Vegas Cyclery and waited for the others to re-turn.

The rest of the group returned soon afterwards. When Jimmy Choi rolled in, he stopped by the curb and put out his left foot to balance himself on his bike. I couldn't help but notice that the muscles in his right arm were twitching a great deal and his right hand still grasped the handlebar of his bike firmly. I asked him, "Which is your Parkinson's dominant hand?" He replied, "It's my right. Sometimes after a ride like this, I can't let go of the handlebar for five minutes." Yet he had a huge smile on this face. Typical of a "PD Hero." Even though the activity put him through a tremendous amount of pain, nothing would have pre-vented him from taking part and making the most of time spent together with a great group of kindred spirits on an absolutely gorgeous day.

Then I spoke with Davis Phinney, asking him how his ride had been. He, too, was displaying an ear-to-ear grin. It had been a great ride. He said that he had hung in with the lead pack, though his wife, Connie, began pulling away. At one point, Carl Ames decided to chase down a group of young people during the last climb to the summit. Davis said, "I can see why his nick-name is 'Bolt'." Just like Jimmy, Davis was reveling in having had a terrific day doing what he has loved all his life – riding a bike. Like many of the riders, he may not be as fast as he once was, but he still derives tremendous joy from being out on two wheels.

I am so grateful to Cidney and Pat for inviting me to this event, to my group of Guardian Angels for their patience in staying with me despite my slow pace, and for everyone else who turned out that day for making me feel that I was an equal member of the group. We were all united on that day in our effort to rise above the limitations that Parkinson's has placed on us and simply enjoy a wonderful ride with friends.

My pace may have been at my personal "Bike Speed" for that day, but I can honestly say that I have shared the road with Olympic medalists at least once in my life.

PD Heroes – Edie Anderson – Roanoke, VA

Edie Anderson with Davis Phinney

Edie Anderson is a Davis Phinney Foundation Ambassador. She has been living with Parkinson's since 2013, diagnosed at age 60. She teaches at a variety of support groups and other Parkinson's educational events about developing a proactive approach to wellness. Edie describes herself as a workout junkie and says that she has "benefitted physically, mentally, and emotionally from my active lifestyle." She wants to give hope to people living with Parkinson's and their caregivers by telling her story and showing that "exercise works to improve our ability to function, which translates into a happier life for all of us."

Edie is a tiny pixie of a gal, but is formidable in her boxing classes. She aggressively "fights back" against PD with all her might.

Edie draws upon her lifelong skills as an educator to share information with people with Parkinson's and their caregivers. She has developed her own PD 101 lesson plan to use when providing basic education about the condition and how to deal with it. One unique method that she uses is to ask a group to describe what a person with PD looks like. They will often describe an old man who is all hunched over. Then she informs them that the "face" of Parkinson's has changed. There are now many women as well men, plus people of all ages who now live with PD. She then reveals that she has PD and many people are shocked because her tremor is fairly mild. It's information sharing such as this that truly is expanding awareness about Parkinson's.

Edie is a great example of choosing to live well today.

CHAPTER 15

Ride With Larry Film Festivals

Ride With Larry – Orlando Anniversary Rides 2012 and 2013

A year after the official Ride With Larry, a group of Larry's friends organized a one-day, 50-mile anniversary ride in South Dakota. I wasn't able to fit in a trip to South Dakota, so I organized an event in Orlando with friends from Commute Orlando and Cycling Savvy. Keri Caffrey created a route called the "Great Loop" and nicknamed it RWL2 (Ride With Larry 2 – Orlando version.) It was exactly 50 miles, starting at the Cady Way trailhead in Orlando, heading north through Winter Park, Maitland, Altamonte Springs, and Heathrow, turning east to Lake Mary, Winter Springs, and Oviedo, then southwest back through Orlando to the original starting point. Nine riders took part and had a great time. On Saturday, June 29, 2013, 19 Orlando cyclists gathered to commemorate the third anniversary of the Ride With Larry (RWL3 – Orlando).

I had learned about the benefits of cycling as therapy. My neurologist (a Parkinson's specialist) agrees that my bike riding has helped slow the progression of my symptoms. My goal is to ride about 100 miles per month. That being said, my mileage had been down a bit leading up to RWL3 due to a heavy work travel schedule and a lot of afternoon rainstorms. For cyclists, nothing beats time in the saddle to stay in top condition or prepare for a long ride. I have to admit, I wasn't as prepared as I would have liked for this 50-mile route. My daughter, Jen Everland, agreed to join me for the ride. She had taken the Cycling Savvy class in March and a week later we completed the 25-mile route of the Orlando Tour de Cure Diabetes Awareness Ride. Jen had decided in advance to do 25 miles of RWL3 and then drop her bike off at my house, which coincided with the midpoint. A wise move on her part.

Jen and I arrived at the Cady Way Trailhead about 7:00 a.m. the day of the ride. Just before we made the last turn, an unusually shaped yellow vehicle passed us going the opposite direction. We unloaded our bikes and got set up for the start. The yellow vehicle rolled in as well and turned out to be a velomobile, a human-powered vehicle (HPV) enclosed in an aerodynamic shell. Fred from Daytona Beach owns this "WAW" model and had towed it behind his electric car. He had gotten slightly turned around before arriving at the starting point. The 19 of us certainly represented a cross-section of cycling options – the WAW, three Catrike three-wheeled tadpole trikes, a Bacchetta two-wheeled recumbent, two Electra Townies, a RANS crank-forward bicycle, and eleven more traditional road and mountain bikes. Quite a sight to behold, and a delight to view as noted by the many positive comments that our group received from on-lookers throughout the day.

The beginning of the ride was reminiscent of the previous year's ride. We were on our way shortly after 7:30 a.m. to take advantage of the cooler morning temperatures and get in as many miles as possible before the rain that had been predicted for the day. The group made its way northbound through Orlando, Winter Park, Maitland, and Altamonte Springs. The streets were virtually empty and we were able to ride two abreast most of the way, which allowed for lots of pleasant conversation. Fred missed out on most of that since he's quite isolated once the cover for the WAW is in place. I rode next to Jen and also spent some time chatting with Dave, the Marketing Director for Catrike.

About 20 minutes later we arrived at the location of the newly installed Ride With Larry painting, the work of local artist Jeff Sonksen. I had asked Jeff to paint a mural commemorating the original Ride With Larry and he graciously agreed to do so, installing it on the fence along the trail a few weeks before our RWL3 ride. Everyone was thrilled to see the finished work and pose with it for photos. The mural of Larry is placed between one of Steve Jobs and Paul Newman, just a few of the hundreds of paintings along the trail.

Jen split off as planned after we arrived at the halfway point. I was so proud of her for being part of this ride. I felt good at that point, though will admit to being tempted to call it a day as well since I was less than a quarter-mile from home. However, I rode on and mentally assessed my status – my legs felt good, breathing was relaxed and easy, I didn't feel particularly overheated, but was beginning to develop pain in the ball of my right foot.

That was a flare-up of Metatarsalgia (also known as "stone bruise"), which had been a problem when I did my first metric century (100 km) on the Ride 4 Ronald ride last September. Extra padding and two pairs of socks had helped up to this point, but were proving to not be enough protection.

We crossed Highway 17-92 on the Cross-Seminole Trail and I got some assistance getting up that incline with a push on the back from Larry Gies. He had been one of my Guardian Angels on the previous year's RWL2 and the Ride 4 Ronald, continuously coaching and encouraging me. He jumped right back into that role on this day. Little did I know how many "Angels" would come to my aid that afternoon. The group stopped for lunch at Tijuana Flats at the Winter Springs Town Center. I knew from the previous year that I wouldn't be very hungry, so I only ordered a small plate of rice and beans. I found that I couldn't eat more than one bite – which I probably should have taken as a sign of dehydration. We'd travelled about 30 miles and I hadn't completely drained my 70 oz. Camelbak. I should have consumed about twice that amount of electrolyte-infused water by that point. The mantra "Drink before you're thirsty" began to play in my head.

As we gathered to resume our ride, Marty Smith, a person whom I had just met, made an extraordinary gesture. He offered to let me ride his Catrike. He'd heard that my foot was hurting and figured that the different riding position would take some of the pressure off of it. I gladly accepted the opportunity – both to help relax my foot and because Catrikes are just so much fun to ride! Marty recently moved from Connecticut to Central Florida and happened to see the RWL3 Event on the Commute Orlando website. I sincerely appreciate him making the exchange, and do believe that he had some fun trying out my Townie as well. It took all of two seconds to become familiar with Marty's Catrike Villager and I was back in business. Switching to the recumbent for

about fifteen miles certainly helped me complete the entire route.

Being at "street level," it was only natural to ride next to another Catrike operator, Mark Egeland. Not only is Mark an overall cycling enthusiast, he is also a Partner and General Manager of BIG CAT Human Powered Vehicles, LLC – the company that designs, manufactures and markets Catrikes. The company was founded in Winter Garden and recently moved their production facility to Orlando. Mark and I had plenty to talk about. I first became familiar with Catrike during the original RWL in South Dakota. Larry Smith rides a Catrike because it is more stable than a two-wheeled bike. One of Mark's dealers, Harlan Krueger from Harlan's Bike and Tour in Sioux Falls, South Dakota, took part in the ride and helped members of the Parkinson's community become familiar with the ease and fun of operating these nimble buggies during test rides. We talked about the upcoming release of the Ride With Larry documentary. We also talked about Ataxia, another neurological illness that affects balance. My knowledge of that disease was very limited until I read some posts by Richard Wharton, owner of Cycling Center, Dallas, and a Cycling Savvy instructor. Richard had coached Emily Penn, who is living with Ataxia, to complete a 25-mile ride on her Catrike. Mark knew Emily well and was wearing a Ride Ataxia jersey to show his support for her efforts and others battling that disease.

While we were gabbing about a whole variety of topics, Mark was taking his place as another of my Guardian Angels. When we approached the second-to-last bridge – one that I had walked my bike over last year, Mark coached me through the set up and rode through it with me with words of encouragement. Going up the final Cady Way Trail Bridge over SR 434, he helped push me to the top – right at a point when my energy was waning. Mark Egeland is just an overall good guy. He loves life and is running a company that is having an incredibly positive affect on many lives. I'm honored to now consider him a friend. That's what happens when you share an experience like riding 50 miles together.

Support came from so many of the other riders throughout the day. For example, I had been on some First Friday Rides with Keith McLane before, and he remembered my mentioning that my son, Brian, had graduated from the University of Southern California, as Keith had. For this ride, Keith elected to wear a USC kit. At one point, I passed him and simply stated USC's motto, "Fight On!" in appreciation for his being part of the ride.

With about seven miles to go, I swapped rides again with Marty and mounted my trusty Townie for the final section. The time on the Catrike had provided the relief that my foot needed, but dehydration and overall fatigue was quickly settling in. I was sliding back in the line and beginning to mentally doubt if I could make it the rest of the way.

Right at that critical point, Keri Caffrey dropped back from her lead position, placing her bike directly in front of me and simply said calmly, "Stay on my wheel." We had picked up a headwind, so she was allowing me to draft off her, but more importantly gave me a singular point of focus. I blocked out everything else around me but her back tire. It was as if the ultimate Top Gun pilot was leading a comrade with three out of four engines burned out back to the landing strip. Keri has been my mentor and friend ever since I took the Cycling Savvy class. She is one of the strongest and smartest cyclists I know. She said "follow her" – so that's what I was going to do.

We were soon joined by Lisa Walker, another one of my heroes. There was no way that I could fail at this point as long as I followed these two. Keri knows what I am capable of, so as we rolled into the final mile she quietly stated, "We're going to pick up the pace now." We began to pull ahead of the group. Then she said, "Bring us home" and with my last bit of energy I sprinted for the finish line. The Davis Phinney Foundation's

motto is "Every Victory Counts." Completing this 50-mile ride, on this day, with three and a half years of Parkinson's under my belt, was indeed a personal victory. However, a victory – like so many – that I accomplished with the help of my friends and love of my family.

John and Keri

Ride With Larry – Film Festival Premiers 2013

RWL – International Release

The first film festival that the RWL film makers entered was the Monterey International Film Festival in Monterey, Mexico. Director Ricardo Villarreal hails from this town and still has family there, so it was a perfect fit. The film was booked for three screenings. From the very first time that it was shown, the theater was packed. It proved so popular that the organizers arranged for a fourth screening. Ride With Larry was awarded with the Best Documentary Film Award.

Ride With Larry – United States Premiere

In September 2013, the US premiere of the film was scheduled to take place in Larry Smith's hometown of Vermillion as part of the South Dakota Film Festival. I was fortunate to be able to return to Vermillion for that screening. Just like the final day of the original ride, the entire town turned out to support Larry and Betty and delight in watching the film together for the first time on the big screen. The honored couple received a standing ovation before the film began and after it finished. While everyone was focused on the film, people were poking each other throughout the movie as they recognized fellow residents such as the local pharmacist and doctor who had made the final cut.

Larry and Betty Smith, and her niece, Katie Skow Villarreal (one of the film's producers) answered questions after the screening. Among the questions asked of her was: "Were there any particular surprises that you experienced once the film was completed?" She said that she had always known that her aunt and uncle had a very special relationship, but was pleased to see the support that they gave to each other. She said, "This truly is a love story, and not just a triumph-over-a-challenge film."

The film won the South Dakota Film Festival 2013 Jury Award for Most Inspiring Film.

Margarita Ride – Vermillion, South Dakota

The day after the Vermillion screening, there was a local bike event called the Margarita Ride. This was not affiliated with the RWL movie, just a coincidence as far as timing. I had asked Betty Smith if Larry was planning to take part in the ride and she said that he wasn't. I asked if Larry might allow me to use his Catrike for the ride and he agreed. I went to their house early the morning of the ride to allow time for a friend to adjust the pedals on the Catrike. When he was finished, he asked me to clip in to the pedals. When I lifted my foot up, he said, "You have the wrong kind of cleats."

Technically, my bike shoes are outfitted with SPD (Shimano Pedaling Dynamics), which are used by 90% of cyclists. It turns out that Larry's pedals were a different type. That potentially would have eliminated my opportunity to take part in the ride. Larry's wife, Betty, offered a solution. She asked what size shoes I wore. Larry's shoes were only a half-size larger, so I tried them on and they fit reasonably well. I was going to be riding not only on the man's bike, but wearing his shoes. That made for a very special day.

I rode from Larry and Betty's house with some of their friends to downtown Vermillion, which was about five miles away. Kevin Brady, a professor at the University of South Dakota and a participant in the full five-day Ride with Larry, gave instructions to the riders prior to releasing us for the day. I had elected to do the 30-mile route and would be accompanied by Odie Mason (also a five-day RWL participant) and Kathryn Keane. We rode on fairly empty roads throughout the back country west of Vermillion for about ten miles before stopping at a local bar for refreshments. It was great to meet some of the other people who were on the ride.

Odie and Kathryn were added to my list of Guardian Angels for their patience and encouragement throughout the day. As we made a turn onto Highway 19, the area became familiar. I knew that was the busy two-lane road with the one large hill before we arrived at the outskirts of town. I asked Kathryn if that hill was coming up soon and she told me that it was a fun one. It had taken every last bit of energy for me to climb it during the original Ride With Larry. However, having the full range of 30 gears to choose from made the ascent a bit easier. It had been a fun ride in which I met a number of new people. Riding Larry Smith's Catrike was a genuine treat. I thanked him for allowing me to use his personal ride when I returned to his house. He was pleased that it had been put to good use for the day.

Ride With Larry – Orlando Film Festival 2013

RWL film Director Ricardo Villarreal asked me to write a note to the organizers of the Orlando Film Festival as a testimonial to help get it selected for that event. I'm not sure whether my note was instrumental or not, but the movie was accepted and given a screening date on the final day of the festival.

I reached out to my cycling friends in the Orlando area and invited them to join me for a bike parade to the screening of Ride With Larry at the Orlando Film Festival. About 20 riders gathered north of town at Retro City Cycles. My daughter, Jen, and I parked near the Plaza Cinema downtown and rode up to the starting point. Cycling Savvy founders Keri Caffrey and Mighk Wilson took part in the ride as well as Cycling Savvy Instructors Lisa Walker and Keith McLane. We rode right down Orange Avenue to the theater and even made the local nightly news.

RWL producer Katie Skow Villarreal came to town for the screening. The theater was fairly packed for the showing and the audience stayed for the Q&A session afterwards, which Katie and I handled. It was clear that everyone liked the film a great deal.

My wife, Laura, and I stayed afterwards for the awards ceremony. We waited with Katie, Mark Egeland from Catrike, and his wife, Heidi Behr. The wait was well worth it because Ride With Larry received two honors that evening: Audience Choice Award and Most Inspirational Film. It was very exciting to see the film recognized to such a high degree.

Ride With Larry – Tampa Film Festival 2014

My letter-writing campaign continued and RWL was selected for the 2014 Gasparilla International Film Festival in Tampa, FL. Ricardo flew in for that event and was pleased to have a packed house for the screening. The film won the Documentary Feature Audience Choice Award.

Ride With Larry – Cleveland Film Festival 2014

The last film festival that I personally attended was in Cleveland, Ohio. That is my hometown and it was a special treat to see the film with my brother, Chuck, who lives in the area. There were two screenings, and both had a full house. In fact, people lined up a half-hour early to make sure that they could get a seat. Both screenings played to a full house.

While the film did not earn an award at this festival, it was extremely well received by the audiences who did see it. Many wanted to know when they could buy a copy. That would take until the fall of 2016 when it became available to purchase on Amazon.com. There are many details to work out when producing a film, such as obtaining music rights, etc., which kept this one unreleased longer than planned.

Ride With Larry – Medical Marijuana

One of Larry Smith's symptoms, which is obvious to those who watch the film, is dyskinesia. That is, a distortion in performing voluntary movements, which often occurs as a side effect of long-term therapy with the medication Carbidopa-Levodopa. Since Parkinson's is a degenerative disease, over time more medication is required to control Parkinson's symptoms.

In addition to their home in South Dakota, Larry and Betty also own a home in California, a state that allows patients with a doctor's prescription to purchase medical marijuana. Larry had reached a point where his medication was no longer controlling his symptoms, in spite of the fact that he had also had Deep Brain Stimulation surgery. (More on this procedure later.) They made the decision to try medical marijuana, which was difficult because Larry was a former police captain and Betty was concerned that even though it was legal in California, it was still not legal throughout the country.

A portion of the film follows Larry from his meeting with a doctor to obtain a prescription, visits an approved medical marijuana dispensary, and records on tape the first time he tried this treatment in the form of an essential oil. Interspersed are well-balanced interviews with leading researchers on the topic. The footage of Larry taking a dose of medical marijuana is incredibly compelling. He goes from having a severe bout of dyskinesia, with his arms flailing and his eyes tightly closed, to being completely relaxed and his eyes wide open and alert within three to four minutes. Anyone who has ever doubted the positive affect of medical marijuana will be impressed by this scene.

In 2016, the filmmakers posted the portion of the Ride With Larry film that focused on medical marijuana on Facebook. The total segment is six minutes, so they released three two-minute clips. Those videos have been viewed over 300 MILLION times!

PD Heroes – Super Support People

It takes an army of incredible, generous people who work tirelessly to increase awareness about Parkinson's and fundraise to help find a cure. One of the strongest networks is Team Fox, who donate their time, energy, and sweat to ensure that a number of events go smoothly. Here are just a few of the stellar volunteers.

Yoko Bradford – Chicago, IL

Yoko is a FOJ (Friend of Jimmy's), as in Jimmy Choi. She caught the running bug and runs a lot of races to benefit Team Fox. In addition, she does a ton of behind-the-scenes work to support Jimmy and Cherry Choi's *Shake It Off 5K*, a Chicago-area fundraiser, each year. When Yoko takes part in a race, she asks people to sponsor one of her "Miles of Smiles" because her smile is infectious and she smiles through any pain she may encounter during a race because she knows that it's for a good cause.

Yoko is constantly running and training. She is enrolled with Charity Miles, which makes a donation in her name to Team Fox for all of the miles that she records through their website.

Crystal Duran – Chicago, IL

Crystal is also a FOJ and, essentially Yoko's "partner in crime" and running buddy. She, too, has completed a great number of races to support Team Fox, and helps out every year at the *Shake It Off 5K.*

Crystal is a school teacher by trade, and another tremendous Team Fox supporter.

Rose Lackey Babcock – Kissimmee, FL

Rose is a physical therapist, specializing in the treatment of Parkinson's disease. Both her father and mother-in-law have PD. Rose runs a local support group, is an approved PWR! Instructor, and serves on the board of the Parkinson's Association of Central Florida.

Rose and her husband, Chris, are also strong supporters of Team Fox. They are the "host family" to many folks from out of town who come to Orlando to run in the Walt Disney World "Dopey Challenge" (a series of races held over four days, consisting of a 5K, 10K, half marathon, and a full marathon.) There is always a strong Team Fox showing at these events, with Rose and Chris cheerfully setting the pace. They have also run the New York City Marathon with Jimmy Choi and other Team Fox members.

Each summer, Rose and Chris put on a "Pints for Parkinson's" fundraising event at a local brew pub. They obtained donated kegs from craft brewers in the area and solicit a large collection of items to be raffled off throughout the event. It's though the efforts of people like Rose and Chris that a Cure for PD will be found.

151

Jennifer Otero – Jacksonville, FL

Jennifer's mother lived with Parkinson's. In her honor, Jennifer created the *First Coast 5K Walk and Run*. The event has grown each year and is the premier PD support vehicle in Jacksonville area.

Jennifer also works with the medical team at the University of Florida — Jacksonville in organizing an annual PD Symposium to increase awareness and provide information about Parkinson's.

PD is not Jennifer's "day job," but she has made it her life's passion.

CHAPTER 16

Super Sprint Triathlons

University of Florida – TriGators Super Sprint Triathlon 2013

My daughter, Jen Everland, took part in a "couch to 5K" program following the birth of her first child, our granddaughter Lilly. I would accompany her on my bike during some of her training sessions, pulling Lilly along in a baby trailer. She continued to take part in several other runs including a Color Run, Watermelon Run, and eventually a half marathon.

In 2013, Jen completed the Cycling Savvy class. The very next week she joined me for my second Tour de Cure 25-mile bike ride. We had a great time that day, though it was only 41 degrees at the start of the ride. Jen rode like a champ and never complained. Completing that event together was a great father-daughter moment.

On the ride home, Jen mentioned that she was planning to do a triathlon in a few weeks. That would be at the University of Florida. This was the 10th anniversary of her graduation from UF. I asked if I could at least drive her because I figured that it would take a lot of energy to participate. She explained that this was a

Super Sprint Triathlon, which consisted of a 250-yard swim in a heated pool, a 3.4-mile bike ride and a one-mile run. After hearing that, and realizing that we had just ridden 25 miles, I said, "I think I could do that." She said, "Of course you could." I tried to wiggle out of it by mentioning that I don't run, to which she replied that I could simply walk the mile at the end. I signed up that afternoon, so there would be no turning back.

Jen arrived at my house about 4:30 a.m. the day of the triathlon. I was finishing up loading the bikes on my car and locking them in place. I had moved up to a hitch-mount bike rack by this time, so there was no fear of losing the bikes on the freeway. We arrived in Gainesville about 7:00 a.m. We were the first in line to check in for the event. I was issued a bib with the number 1 on it. I had a feeling that would be the last time that I would be leading the pack the rest of the day. The students at the registration table wrote our number on one leg with a marking pen, and our age on the other. I was proudly displaying "61" for all to see. We took our bikes over to the transition area, which was right in front of the University of Florida football stadium, "The Swamp."

We had quite a while to wait for the start, and to size up our competition. Jen was kind enough to point out that one gentleman had "66" on his leg, though I had to admit that he looked very fit for that age. Neither of us had been able to do much training for the swim portion, so that was our biggest concern. In addition to not being well prepared, I was concerned about how my right shoulder would hold up. I had seen my orthopedic doctor who, based on an MRI, had diagnosed an impingement in my shoulder. That resulted in pain when I raised my arm or tried to rotate it. Basically, arthritis was creating bone spurs that were grinding on each other and causing the shoulder to lock up. He had said, "You'll tell me when it's time to operate." I hadn't reached that point yet, but I worried that the swim might get me there.

As the swim portion began, Jen and I drifted to the back of the line. Once I jumped in the water, I took a few attempts at a crawl stroke. My right shoulder was not having any of that movement. So, I tucked my right arm to my chest and completed the five laps of 50 yards each using only my left arm or a modified doggie paddle. It was slow going and I was the last person out of the pool.

I gained a lot of respect for the term "transition." Parkinson's causes a person to be a bit slower in their movements, so the simple act of putting on my socks and bike shoes seemed ridiculously slow. The younger competitors jogged effortlessly from the pool area to their bikes, while I did a slow shuffle. The good news was that I had completed the swim and I hadn't drowned. Jen had finished ahead of me, so I knew that she was already doing her bike ride.

Arriving at my bike, I put on my helmet and gloves and then walked my bike to the road. We weren't allowed to mount our bikes until we passed the front of the stadium because there were pedestrians in the area. Once I reached the right spot, I hopped on my bike and was in fifth gear before I even got to the street. I knew that this was my strongest section of the day and I planned on attacking it with all I had. As I started heading out on the bike route, a motorcycle policeman pulled up behind me. I realized that he had the assignment of following the last rider – that would be me.

After about a quarter of a mile, Gale Lemerand Drive makes a sharp descent down to Museum Road. I was in my top gear and picking up speed. I glanced down quickly and noticed that I was doing 27 mph, the fastest that I ever recall riding on my trusty Electra Townie. The motorcycle officer shot past me and blocked the intersection so I could set up for a right-hand turn. I moved to the double yellow line and then leaned hard into the turn. If I was going to go down, I was going to make it dramatic. However, it was no problem. I whizzed around the corner and set into a steady pace along Museum Road. Lake Alice – complete with live alligators – came up on my left, then the Bat House flew by on my right.

I made a left on Hull Road and was cruising along at a steady pace. I took a few swigs of water from my Camelbak to stay hydrated, but was feeling good. By the time I made the next left onto Mowry Road, I was beginning to feel "the burn" from racing. I was definitely pushing myself more than my normal pace. The last turn was back onto Gale Lemerand Drive. Then it struck me – that hill that was so fun to ride down had to be climbed on the final leg of the bike route. The motorcycle policeman was riding right next to me. I imagined that he was talking to his buddies on his radio, placing bets that I would stop or drop out of the race. I wasn't going to let that happen. I caught the light at Museum Road and began the ascent. I downshifted at just the right time, however I needed to go all the way down to first gear. There was nowhere else to go, except for my internal "Little Engine That Could" gear. I was NOT going to stop, quit, or put my foot down. I was tempted at one point, but I kept hearing the purring of that Harley Davidson next to me and focused on simply putting one pedal stoke in front of the other. The Swamp came into view, and before I knew it, I had completed the bike ride section. The motorcycle officer turned around before I could thank him, but in my mind I added him to my list of

Guardian Angels. Not sure if he won or lost his bet with his friends, but I was the big winner in my own heart at that point.

After kicking off my bike shoes and putting on my sneakers, I began the final mile. Students from the TriGators Club were posted to guide us along the "run" section. I told the first one that I saw, "I left it all on the bike route." He began to walk with me. The next student guide joined in. I ended up with about six students in tow, encouraging me and walking with me to the finish line. I delivered an impromptu lecture on Parkinson's and informed them about the benefits of exercise to PD patients. Since some of them were studying Exercise Physiology, perhaps that didn't fall on deaf ears. At least they were polite enough to listen.

When I was just about to make the final turn, one of the students

said to me, "You have to run the last 50 yards." That was the pathway that leads to the front of the Ben Hill Griffin Stadium. I mustered all of my remaining strength and burst into a jog. Jen was waiting for me at the finish line and snapped a few photos of me completing my first Super Sprint Triathlon. We celebrated our joint victories and were both very proud of each other. I officially came in last place, but I did it and it felt great.

University of Florida – TriGators Super Sprint Triathlon 2015

In January 2014, I had a total right shoulder replacement surgery. It took five months of hard work to completely rehabilitate the shoulder, but it was well worth it. My shiny new titanium shoulder works like a charm. I am very grateful to the team of physical therapists at Ability Rehabilitation in Lake Mary for the encouragement, prodding, and support.

In 2015, I decided to once again join my daughter for the Super Sprint Triathlon. However, this time I decided to prepare myself by joining the local YMCA in Lake Mary. I was a bit hesitant swimming the first lap in the pool, but ended up swimming 250 yards effortlessly during my first workout. While far from heavy-duty training, I knew that I would be much better prepared for my second time around.

At the event itself, the swim portion was much more enjoyable in 2015. Once again, I was the last person out of the water, yet I felt good about my swim. The bike ride was almost a duplicate of the previous time, including having my own personal motorcycle escort. I didn't end up with an entourage of students for the walk this time, but had a pleasant stroll for the last mile. At one point, I noticed that the sun was behind me and casting a

perfect shadow in front of me. I took out my phone and captured an interesting video which showed my left arm and hand in full tremor mode, with my left arm hanging down at my side since it hadn't swung properly for the past few years – another symptom of Parkinson's.

Jen and I celebrated just as much after the 2015 Triathlon. I still came in last, but we both had achieved a personal record) compared to our first attempt. Another challenge conquered, another victory for each of us.

PD Heroes – Boxing for Parkinson's

Boxing has become a popular activity amongst the PD crowd. A program called Rock Steady Boxing was developed in 2006 by former Marion County (Indiana) Prosecutor, Scott C. Newman, who is living with Parkinson's. It caught on like wildfire. There are 343 Rock Steady Boxing programs around the world, training about 17,150 people with Parkinson's. This non-contact boxing-based fitness curriculum allows boxers to condition for optimal agility, muscular endurance, accuracy, hand-eye coordination, footwork, and overall strength to defend against and overcome opponents. In this case, however, Parkinson's

159

disease is the opponent. Exercises vary in purpose and form but share one common trait: they are rigorous and intended to extend the perceived capabilities of the participant.

I tried and very much enjoyed participating in boxing classes. In addition to a great workout, there's something very satisfying about "fighting back against Parkinson's."

For myself, boxing doesn't appear to be a long-term solution since the bouncing around tends to aggravate some degenerative discs in my back. However, I was very impressed by a couple of gentlemen in my class who participated even though they had to use walkers for balance and stability. Some people modify the exercise by doing it sitting down. Those folks aren't rolling over and letting Parkinson's get the better of them. They are taking responsibility for their own health and wellbeing.

PD Heroes – Natasha McCarthy – Prince Edward Island, Canada

Natasha is a mother of two girls who was diagnosed with Young Onset Parkinson's disease at age 36 in September, 2013. Her daughters are still just ages nine and five-and-a-half. Considering the fact that her husband travels extensively for work, Natasha has her work cut out for her in caring for the girls and keeping the home fires burning for her husband. She went from working and feeling healthy to being in pain with Dystonia, being slouched over, and having difficulty doing simple tasks. Her illness forced her to give up her job and deal with more issues than a young person should have to face.

However, Natasha has fought back in many ways. She recognizes the importance of exercising and takes advantage of a number of activities, including group exercise classes, boxing, and even horseback riding. It's not unusual to see her post photos of herself jumping horses or even standing balanced on the back of a moving horse.

To keep her cognitive skills sharp, Natasha writes, performs, and records music. She plays several instruments, her favorite being the fiddle. She built a music corner in her garage, and friends drop by to jam together. Her daughters are beginning to learn to play piano and guitar. This also brings great joy to Natasha and helps her block out some of the challenges that she faces.

Natasha writes a blog entitled, "A Broken Body's Journey." Her blogging earned her a spot as a World Parkinson Congress Ambassador for the Portland conference in September 2016. That was where I met Natasha in person. From photos she'd posted, I knew to be on the lookout for the girl with blue hair, and found her one morning while waiting for a session to begin. She was just as sweet and authentic as her writing had reflected.

Her most recent effort to "push back PD" was a bicycle ride with a couple of other Parkies across Prince Edward Island, Canada. After the ride in June, Natasha wrote, "Last week I set out on a journey of a lifetime with two Parkie friends and together we achieved something I never expected I would in my wildest dreams without having Parkinson's, let alone with it. Myself, Dan Steele and Paul Bernard cycled Prince Edward Island's Confederation trail from tip to tip totaling 273 km in 5 days to raise awareness and funds for Parkinson's! We called ourselves the PEI Pedaling Parkies!

We spent over 20 hours in the saddle, we biked through extreme heat, wind and rain. There were times I honestly did not think I could go on and oddly enough every time that happened I saw a butterfly right in front of me, leading the way. I've written about butterflies before and their significance to me. They symbolize a catalytic moment in life and when a butterfly breaks open its cocoon to take flight, the harder its struggle is to get free, the stronger it will be in flight and the longer it will live. I do not believe in coincidences and in the moments I thought I couldn't pedal one more turn, there was a reason a bright yellow butterfly would appear just ahead of my tire, fluttering forward. A reminder to keep going!"

CHAPTER 17

Inspiration

Daily PD Warriors

The individuals described in the PD Heroes vignettes have been a genuine inspiration to me as I've come to know them throughout my journey with Parkinson's. If asked, each would simply say that they were doing their best to stay ahead of the disease and had never intended to stand out. However, the way that they choose to live their lives does set them apart from the average person.

Courage doesn't apply only to completing marathons or finishing lengthy races. Sometimes it is simply refusing to give up. I equally admire the individuals who just get out of bed every day, or take a walk around the block, or ride their bike for one mile. Choosing to participate in those activities for certain people takes genuine courage. Those PD Warriors are as impressive as anyone I have described throughout the book.

People have told me that I have inspired them. If anything that I have done has inspired another person, particularly one who is making the best of their lives while dealing with Parkinson's, then I feel very gratified. I have often been told that I am a connector – someone who brings people together or helps people find resources that they need at a certain point in their lives. That is no doubt a God-given skill or talent that I possess and I derive great enjoyment from carrying out my role as a connector. If someone else's journey is a bit smoother because I introduced them to a person or program that provides them with information or encourages them to be more active, then I feel that I am fulfilling one of my life's purposes.

After hearing about my early bike riding adventures, people will often ask me, "Are you riding as much these days?" A couple of life events slowed me down a bit, including the need for a total shoulder replacement and subsequent six months of rehab, gall bladder removal surgery, and several degenerative discs in my back. However, all of those were temporary issues that sidelined me for only a short while. I have participated more in the local PWR! classes and done less distance cycling. I do have plans to resume a more consistent level of bike riding. I know that it's important in my effort to control my Parkinson's. I also want to serve as a role model to those who hear my story.

After meeting so many PD Heroes who have experienced such amazing accomplishments, I had a brief period where I was getting down, allowing thoughts to enter my mind like, "I'm not doing anything near as ambitious as this person or that person."

Then I came across a sign that read, "Climb Every *Other* Mountain." That spoke directly to me, as if reminding me that I am on my own journey and I don't have to do what another person does. That is their choice for their own journey. If I choose to tackle a particularly challenging goal (by my standards), that should be based on my individuals needs and criteria, not simply because someone else did it. I'm not letting myself off the hook and saying that I'm not going to do anything. Just that the choice is mine and mine alone, as your choices should meet your own objectives.

CHAPTER 18

Deep Brain Stimulation Surgery

University of Florida Movement Disorder Center

My initial Parkinson's disease diagnosis was made by a neurologist in the Orlando area. I was under his care for about three years. While he handled my case with the standard approach, I had my doubts about the extent of his knowledge in areas such as exercise. Early on I had told him about some concerns about falling off my bike while riding on sidewalks. I didn't have a balance issue. I simply needed to be trained to ride on the road. He recommended that I confine my riding to a stationary bike in the gym. I disregarded his advice. By the time I had ridden 3,000 miles, and finally converted him to appreciating the benefit of exercise, I decided it was time to make a change in terms of my Parkinson's care.

I had been hearing about the value of seeing a Movement Disorder Specialist. That is a neurologist who has taken advanced training in the treatment of Parkinson's disease. The best program in my area is at the University of Florida Center for Movement Disorders and Neurorestoration in Gainesville, FL. I obtained a referral from my local doctor and scheduled an appointment for October, 2013. My local neurologist changed my medication to Carbidopa-Levodopa (Sinemet) prior to that appointment. Sinemet is considered the "gold standard" of Parkinson's medications. First developed in 1967, it is one way to conclusively determine a diagnosis of Parkinson's. If Sinemet works, the patient "has it." I passed that test. Going on this medication was a requirement prior to being accepted as a patient at UF.

My first appointment at UF consisted of four separate meetings. The first was with my assigned neurologist, Dr. Irene Malaty. Coincidentally, John Gabriel with the Parkinson Association of Central Florida Board also was being seen by her and had described her as an "angel sent from heaven." For that appointment, I had to be off my PD medications for my symptoms to be the most pronounced. Dr. Malaty met with me for an hour and a half. She was the most genuinely concerned, empathetic, and kind doctor that I had ever met. I knew that I would be well cared for by her. I must admit, I had to concur with John Gabriel's assessment as well.

Next, I met with a physical therapist, Meredith DeFranco. She put me through a battery of tests and asked about my level of activity. She was thrilled to hear about my bike riding and encouraged me to not only keep that up, but to get involved in additional forms of exercise.

My next meeting was with an occupational therapist, Lisa Warren. She, too, tested me, but with a different focus than the physical therapist. One test involved turning over 16 wooden pegs on a board. The task was to pick each one up, flip it over and return it to a hole in the board. Child's play, right? It turned out to be a very humbling experience. I couldn't believe how long it took me to do this simple activity. My local neurologist had told me that I was developing some rigidity, but didn't explain what that meant. This exercise clearly showed me what rigidity is all about. I didn't have a stiff shoulder, but in my case rigidity presented itself as a decrease in fine motor skills. Seeing the results of completing the task with my left hand (my Parkinson's dominant side) compared to my right hand actually brought me to tears. It wasn't "woe is me, I have this terrible disease," but rather "I finally understand why I can't get my wallet out of my back pocket or I fumble with removing my keys from my front pocket." Lisa also observed that my right shoulder, while not currently affected by Parkinson's or presenting rigidity, did have an impingement and suggested that I consult my orthopedic surgeon. I did so and had a total shoulder replacement a few months later. Lisa offered a number of tips to help me prevent falls and to improve my flexibility despite the rigidity.

The last meeting that day was with a speech therapist. Many people with Parkinson's experience softer than normal speech patterns or difficulty swallowing. I did not have either of those problems at that time, but it was useful to complete a series of vocal exercises to set a baseline for the future. That was an interesting appointment. A graduate student was conducting the exam. She asked if it would be alright if some students sat in on the session. I agreed. Initially, there were three young ladies, in addition to the female graduate student in the examining room with me, listening to me sing, shout, and perform other tests. Two or three more female students joined during the session. Finally, one more came in, and I realized that while she looked as young as the rest, she was the actual doctor. It seemed as if I was sitting in a room with an entire sorority. After the graduate student completed her tests, I asked the doctor if I could share some information about PD and exercise. She agreed, then got all excited as I shared my stories. She went out and grabbed a video camera and recorded me telling my stories. I've probably been a part of the Parkinson's training for UF speech therapy students ever since.

The interdisciplinary approach used by the University of Florida provides a much better approach to monitoring and treating patients over time. Initially, I saw the neurologist, Dr. Malaty, every six months, and some of the other specialists about once a year. Since UF is a teaching hospital, I would often be seen by a Resident prior to seeing Dr. Malaty. They would conduct an exam, then discuss their observations with her, and then she would meet with me to review the results. The focus at UF is genuinely patient-centric. I knew that I had found a new home for my Parkinson's care.

Why Deep Brain Stimulation Surgery Now?

I continued my regular appointments with Dr. Malaty at the University of Florida about every six months for the next three years. The tremor in my left hand and foot increased over time and was addressed by increasing the dosage of Carbidopa-Levodopa. I tolerated the additional medication well. However, I knew that over time there was a risk of side effects such as dyskinesia. I wanted to avoid the involuntary movements that result from dyskinesia if at all possible.

By the spring of 2016, Dr. Malaty and I had a serious conversation about Deep Brain Stimulation (DBS) surgery for the first time. That treatment had originally been considered a "late stage" interaction. Recent research, however, has proven it to be beneficial to patients as early as two or three years following their diagnosis. Patients have described their symptoms as being "rolled back" four or five years following DBS surgery. At that time, I had lived with PD for six and a half years, so that seemed like a logical time for me to consider this option.

Pre-Assessment Process

DBS surgery is not something to be taken lightly, by either the patient or the medical team. Prospective patients need to be assessed to ensure that they are viable candidates for the operation. The medical team wants to know whether the person will tolerate the procedure well and that the symptoms the patient wants to control will be best served by this intervention. Symptoms such as tremor, rigidity, and dystonia (involuntary tightening of muscles) respond very well to DBS, while balance and freezing are not relieved much at all.

The University of Florida has a convenient way to evaluate each DBS candidate through a pre-assessment Process called "Fast Track." It involves two to two-and-a-half days of appointments with the entire medical team. That includes the neurosurgeon, neurologist, physical therapist, occupational therapist, speech therapist, psychiatrist, neuro-psychologist, and social worker. The entire team meets to discuss their individual observations after the assessments have taken place. Each person's opinion is considered to determine if DBS is the proper approach for an individual candidate. Only then is the person informed that they have been approved and surgery will be scheduled. I went through the pre-assessment process in mid-May, 2016.

My appointment with my neurosurgeon, Dr. Kelly Foote, was particularly interesting. He started by telling me that I would be about "number 1,250" in terms of the patients on whom he had performed a Deep Brain Stimulation surgery. To say the least, that's well above the average for a neurosurgeon. He has quite a bit of experience, and is ranked as one of the top five neurosurgeons in the world. Next, he told me that a person would have to be crazy to allow someone to cut into their perfectly good brain. He followed that by explaining the risks and benefits of DBS surgery. I agreed that my brain was probably "less than perfect" due to the Parkinson's disease, so the benefits out-weighed the risks. He then proceeded to tell me about the two possible brain regions where he could implant the lead (the end of a wire that connects to a neurostimulation generator). The options are globus pallidus internus (GPI) or the subthalamic nucleus (STN). He asked for input from the two Fellows (Residents receiving advanced training) and it was a lively discussion. Each has its pluses and minuses. Ultimately, STN was selected as the best site for me.

Dr. Foote treated me like a "part of the team" for a successful outcome of this operation, not simply a patient. He even had one of the Fellows pull up an electronic version of the Davis Phinney Foundation "Every Victory Counts" manual and followed the "Deep Brain Stimulation (DBS) Self-Assessment Worksheet." Obviously, Dr. Foote didn't need that guide, but it was incredibly respectful of him to use it considering the fact that he knows of my association with the Foundation. For the question, "What Parkinson's symptoms do you expect to be improved by DBS in order for you to be satisfied with the procedure's outcome?" I replied that they were tremor, rigidity, dystonia, and fatigue. He was able to tell me that the surgery would be able to significantly improve the first three, though it didn't address fatigue. Three out of four is not bad, so I was pleased.

One of the Fellows then explained the surgery in detail to me as follows:

- Since all my symptoms are on my left side, they would implant a lead on the right side of my brain. Each side of the brain controls the opposite side.

- I would have two operations. The first would be to implant the lead in my brain. A month later, the neurostimulation generator (battery) would be implanted in my chest, similar to a heart pacemaker.

- The first procedure would take about five hours and I would be awake the entire time because they would need to communicate with me to make sure that they positioned the lead in the right place.

- The second surgery would be under general anesthetic.

- They would not need to shave my head.

- I would stay overnight in the hospital for one night following the first surgery.

- The second surgery would be on an outpatient basis and I could go home afterwards.

Dr. Foote and his team made me feel very comfortable and confident about the prospective outcome of the surgery.

Most of the other appointments were fairly routine. The neuro-psychiatric evaluations were, to use a phrase, mind-numbing. The technician must have had a two-inch stack of papers to go through with me to assess my cognitive functions. They included everything from lists of numbers and letters to repeat, shapes to draw and then recall an hour later, stories to listen to and repeat immediately and later during the sessions, etc. If you ever want to test your sanity, try going through this process. They even snuck in an extra set of tests in on me, which were part of a study.

About two weeks later, I received a call from Fran with Dr. Foote's office. While they are very serious about their work, they do like to put patients at ease. Fran told me, "Congratulations, you've just won a right-side DBS procedure." My first surgery was scheduled for October 5, 2016.

A Last-Minute Upgrade

About a week before my surgery, I received a phone call from my neurosurgeon, Dr. Kelly Foote, with an unexpected proposition about the device that would be used in my DBS surgery. He explained that for the past twenty years or more, the only company approved in the United States for Deep Brain Stimulation devices was Medtronic. I knew a little bit about Medtronic because friends who had undergone the procedure had all been implanted with that company's device. Dr. Foote explained that another company, St. Jude Medical, had just gained approval from the FDA on September 22, 2016. While he had no problem with Medtronic and had always had good support from their representatives, he said that he was glad to know that there was now competition in this space. He stressed that this was not a clinical trial, they had received full authorization to begin marketing their product. Dr. Foote shared some of the advantages of the St. Jude Medical Infinity DBS System.

First, the multi-directional lead technology had eight leads instead of four in the Medtronic device. That meant more opportunity to customize the therapy to maximize on-times and reduce side effects.

Second, the programming by the doctor's team would use a Bluetooth-controlled wireless iOS software platform on an Apple iPad Mini, and the patient is given an Apple iPod Touch to adjust up to sixteen programmed settings.

Third, the DBS neurostimulation device was the smallest on the market and upgradeable, meaning that new technology can be accessed through a software update without the need for additional surgery.

St. Jude Medical had selected the date of October 5th as the date on which they were hoping to implant the first Infinity DBS system. Dr. Foote explained that he had three surgeries scheduled for that date, and that of the three I was the most viable candidate based on my pre-assessment results. I agreed to go ahead with the St. Jude Medical option, which would make me the first person in the United States to be implanted with the St. Jude Medical Infinity DBS System. (Note: St. Jude Medical was purchased by and became a division of Abbot in January, 2017).

October 5, 2016 – DBS Implant Surgery

My son, Brian, flew in from California on Monday, October 3rd, to be with us for the surgery. Laura and I picked him up at the Orlando International Airport and drove to Gainesville that afternoon. The next day was taken up with pre-op procedures, which included an MRI (fortunately a short one this time) and some blood work and discussions with an anesthesiologist.

I had offered to speak to my occupational therapist's classes several times, but we could never coordinate our calendars. A few weeks before my surgery she said, "That won't work now because you won't be shaking anymore." So, the day before my procedure I had my son videotape me discussing the challenges that a person with Parkinson's faces with everyday tasks such as eating soup, drinking from a cup without spilling, brushing my teeth, and shaving. We posted the video that day and over the next few months it received 21,000 hits on Facebook. Lisa Warren, my OT, said that the students appreciated watching the video as well.

Laura, Brian, and I reported to Shands Hospital at 6:00 a.m. on the day of the operation. After a brief wait, I was taken to the prep area. I noticed about five people near the reception desk when we checked in. They turned out to be a team from St. Jude

175

Medical who were there to observe and assist with the procedure. After changing into a hospital gown, an anesthesiologist checked in with me. He told me, "You will be receiving a bill from my office for my services today, but I won't be giving you anything." Ha! Another funny guy. I knew in advance that I wouldn't be receiving any anesthesia. He did, however, let me know that he and his team would be present for the entire operation and if there was an emergency, they could react immediately to keep me out of pain.

Dr. Foote and some assistants arrived to fit me with a "halo" – a medical device that would keep my head from moving during the surgery and be used to connect guidance equipment to aid the surgeon. As he was putting that on my head, Dr. Foote said,

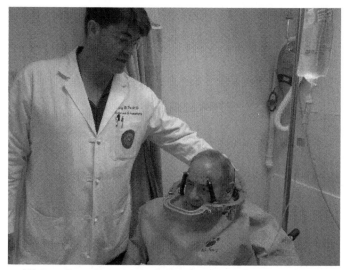

"This will be the most painful part of the entire procedure." Then he proceeded to inject some medication into my scalp in four places and attach the device with four thumb screws. He was correct – that wasn't a lot of fun. I did my best to stay calm during this process, even flashing a smile for a photo taken once the halo was in place. In addition, it was awkward because it limited the mobility of my head. Soon, however, the local anesthetic began to kick in and I felt a bit more comfortable. I was taken to the x-ray wing and placed on a table for a CT scan. The halo was bolted to the table to keep my head from moving. As they did that, it felt like the screws holding the halo to the back of my head sunk in a bit deeper. Fortunately, the CT scan only took a few minutes.

The information from the CT scan was overlapped with the results of the MRI, and Dr. Foote fed that into a computer to "map out" the entire operation. In effect, he does the operation twice – once on the computer, virtually, and again on the patient.

After receiving good wishes from Laura and Brian, I was taken to the operating room. The room was packed with equipment. The St. Jude Medical Team stood off to one side. I was greeted by the other major player in this procedure, Dr. Michael Okun, the neurologist. His part wouldn't take place until later in the operation. He had his own team of about five neurology fellows. Dr. Foote explained how I was to get up on the operating table, which was more like a reclining chair. He told me to stand on a stepstool and then fall backwards – sort of a leap of faith. However, as I did that, he scooped up my legs and personally helped me get into a comfortable position. That was important because I wouldn't be able to move for about five hours. An anesthesiologist was on my right side and other nurses and doctors were on my left.

Dr. Foote stood behind me and placed a covering over the halo, which effectively defused some of the harsh lights shining down on me. Then he went through a checklist, asking me to give my date of birth, confirming the procedure that they were about to do, conducting a roll call of all the participants, and making sure that the DBS device was in the room. Check, check, check, check.

It was comforting to know the care that they take to make sure that everything is ready. Next, Dr. Foote proceeded to wash my hair with an antiseptic shampoo. When he finished, he said, "Now your hair is orange." Rather appropriate since the Florida Gator team colors are orange and blue. He didn't have to shave my head and only snipped away a few hairs.

Then the fun part began. An incision was made on the right side of my head, about two inches long, starting at my front hairline. I didn't feel that because they had numbed the area. At that point, the drilling would commence. Dr. Foote had explained that he would be drilling a hole through my skull about the size of a dime to gain access to my brain. Neither the skull nor brain have nerve endings, so I would not be feeling any pain during this part of the operation. I did, however, hear the drill and felt a bit of pressure when he pushed it against my skull. My mind drifted and I began thinking of things like, "Well, that must be about a 3/8" drill bit." Time to just let me mind go to my happy place.

Throughout the entire procedure, Dr. Foote was talking to me and letting me know what was going on, and what would be taking place next. It was actually rather fascinating. The anesthesiologist talked to me as well, making sure that I was breathing and comfortable. After completing the hole in the skull that provided access to my brain, Dr. Foote then used a device I would describe as a Dremel tool to countersink an area about a quarter-inch deep and the size of a quarter. That held a plastic cap, which would keep the wires in place. As the small drill buzzed away, I heard Dr. Foote ask an assistant to vacuum up the "skull dust." I have to admit, that's the first time I'd ever heard that phrase before. Rather alarming to think of part of your skull being carved into like a jack-o-lantern.

Next, Dr. Foote inserted the lead through the hole that he had made in my skull down into my brain. He nestled it precisely at the predetermined point in the STN region. When he had it just where he wanted it, his "heavy lifting" was done for the day.

At that point, Dr. Okun and his team took over. I realized that I had won the "DBS Lottery" by getting Dr. Foote and Dr. Okun for this operation. They are truly the "Dream Team" based on their knowledge and experience. The role of the neurologist in a DBS operation is to "listen" to the brain. The brain emits electrical signals, and this team converts those to sound waves. By accessing different parts of the brain, they can determine if the leads are in exactly the right position to effectively control the Parkinson's symptoms such as tremor.

To allow the neurologists to focus on their listening, at this point in the operation all the lights in the operating room are turned off except for one light above the patient. That was a truly ethereal moment. While I was the center of attention, the important work was taking place around me on the laptops and over the speakers in the room. The neurology team seemed to be working their way through a grid, calling out sector numbers and listening to see if each area was precisely dialed in to the frequency they desired. At one point, Dr. Okun called out excitedly after hearing one sound pattern, "That sounds just like Led Zeppelin!" In fact, it was a cool sound but he clearly had listened to a different album than I had back in the day. To me, it sounded more like a beached Orca whale.

In between the listening sessions, I was asked to perform some of the Parkinson's agility movements, such as tapping my fingers together, opening and closing my hand quickly, and turning the palm of my hand back and forth. At this point, I had been on the operating table for over three hours. However, I became a bit anxious at one point due to the halo's limited field of view. I motioned one of the Fellows to come closer. She kindly held my hand to reassure me.

Then came the truly exciting part of the operation. I was not allowed to take my Parkinson's medication the day of the surgery. My tremor was evident throughout the operation and some of the staff helped control it by massaging my hand. However, we had reached a critical moment when Dr. Okun announced that they would be applying "power." He told me to expect either a jolt of electricity or a "pulling in my jaw or face." I felt a bit of a buzz in my elbow, which almost immediately subsided. After that, as they made adjustments, I felt the pulling in my jaw and then it would relax. After experiencing this sensation a number of times, with adjustments being made based on my feedback, someone observed that my tremor had, in fact, subsided. I looked down and my hand, arm, and leg were perfectly still and relaxed. It was an amazing and emotional moment.

Dr. Okun was also very excited to program the St. Jude Medical device with his Apple iPad Mini for the first time. Even though the neurostimulation device had not been implanted in my chest at this time, he was able to work through a standalone unit to make adjustments. Several times when he noticed a difference compared to the Medtronic device, he told the rep, "You'll be fixing that, right?" I have to imagine that given his status in the Parkinson medical community, that if Dr. Okun stated a preference, the St. Jude Medical team would do everything possible to comply with his wishes.

With the testing complete and the results having proven to be successful, it was up to Dr. Foote and his team to close up the incision and complete the operation. He works very precisely and requires the same of his assistants. Even the way that he put in the staples to close the wound had to be done in a certain way to minimize leaving a bump in the scalp. He gave specific instructions to his assistant on how to remove the halo, stating that if he didn't support my head properly at this point, I would be impaled on the halo screws and could be expected to let out a blood-curdling scream. This was an important step because my head was hanging over the end of the operating table at that point. The assistant properly followed Dr. Foote's instructions without causing me any pain. Once the halo was removed, I was wheeled to the recovery room.

The total time in the operating room was right around 4½ hours. I was thrilled to see my family again. Laura and Brian had been joined by our daughter, Jen, who drove up from Orlando that morning. They were all relieved that everything had gone so smoothly. I was very thankful that the surgery had gone well and was relatively pain-free. I was also thrilled to have been given a glimpse of what life would be like in the near future when I was completely "powered up" and tremor-free.

Post-Surgery Recovery

The recovery process went quickly due to the fact that I had not been given any anesthetic.

I was taken from the recovery room to a private room on the eleventh floor. It had a great view overlooking "The Swamp" – the University of Florida Stadium. I would have enjoyed the view more if it hadn't been so rainy and windy outside. As it turns out, my operation had taken place a day before Hurricane Matthew was scheduled to make landfall on the State of Florida, and Gainesville was already receiving the outer bands of rain from the approaching storm. I was allowed to go home the next day and Shands Hospital was closed just a few hours later due to the hurricane. My timing had been perfect.

One of the only moments of discomfort throughout the entire procedure and recuperation was being given Oxycodone for pain management because it caused me to become so confused that I couldn't remember what day it was. I discontinued that narcotic after three days and switched to Extra Strength Tylenol to take care of any remaining pain, which was minimal.

Apparently, some people experience a "honeymoon effect" following the implantation of the wire during a DBS surgery. Symptoms such as tremor may be reduced even though steady power is not being applied from a battery source, since the neurostimulation generator has not yet been implanted. I didn't notice much honeymoon effect, though my symptoms were well controlled because my medication remained at the same level as prior to the surgery.

November 4, 2016 – Neurostimulation Generator Implantation

The second operation to implant the neurostimulation generator (aka the battery) took place at the University of Florida Outpatient Surgery Center on November 3, 2016. As opposed to the first surgery, I was given general anesthetic this time, so I don't remember much about the procedure.

During the operation, two additional incisions were made in my scalp to allow Dr. Foote room to place the wire into a channel in my skull. He then threaded the wire down the inside of my neck. He made an incision in my chest and implanted the neurostimulation generator under a layer of muscle. This is similar to the way that a pacemaker is placed into a heart patient's chest. Finally, the wire was connected to the device, the incisions were closed, and I was sent to recovery.

When I woke up in recovery, I first saw my wife, Laura. Dr. Foote and two people from St. Jude Medical were also there. I woke up fairly easily and was alert as Dr. Foote and the reps worked together to establish an initial program for my device using the Apple iPad Mini. There was a bit of testing to adjust the setting to their satisfaction. Once again, I felt some electrical impulses in my arm and some pulling in the muscles during the adjustment process.

After tinkering with the settings for a bit, Dr. Foote declared, "The tremor has been eliminated." That was music to my ears and a genuinely joyful moment.

Laura was able to drive me home that afternoon and the recuperation went smoothly. Incredibly, I actually felt that the second procedure was a bit more invasive than having the wires implanted into my brain. My chest remained a bit sensitive for about a month in the area where they implanted the battery.

During the following week, I began to fully appreciate the results of the Deep Brain Stimulation surgery. As mentioned above, the tremor in my left hand, left arm, and left leg were significantly reduced to the point that I didn't feel like I was shaking at all. I also noticed that my left arm was swinging freely when I walked. That was quite a change, because I had experienced a loss of normal arm swing for the past six years. I also noticed slightly less stiffness in my left hand from the rigidity. Dystonia is a condition that causes an involuntary tightening of muscles. I had experienced that occasionally in my left foot. That seemed a bit better as well.

There was one additional improvement that I hadn't expected. The previous summer, I had begun to have pain in the front of my lower left leg. I sought an opinion from my orthopedic doctor, who ordered an MRI. That showed that I had three degenerative discs in the lumbar region of my back, probably not surprising at my age. He sent me to a pain management specialist and I received a total of three nerve blocks. Each one was quite effective, but wore off fairly quickly. The relief from the third one appeared to last a bit longer. I had the last injection in mid-September. The radicular pain in my lower left leg had subsided from the shots. Soon after that was resolved, I began to experience a sharp pain in my left shoulder blade. I didn't have time to have it examined by the orthopedic doctor prior to the two DBS procedures. However, once the battery was connected, this pain went away. Apparently, that was also a form of dystonia and the DBS surgery eliminated it. Even six months later, this pain has not returned. I chalked up the relief of this back pain as "double bonus points," since I certainly had not expected this issue to be resolved by the DBS intervention.

DBS Programming Sessions

I returned to Gainesville on November 10th, six days after the neurostimulation generator device had been installed. I drove myself the two-and-a-half hours from my home near Orlando the day before and felt great. This was the first of six monthly DBS programming sessions that I would be attending. Over the course of these visits, a highly trained DBS programmer would be adjusting the settings on my DBS device to maximize the positive benefits from the surgery and minimize negative side effects. My programmer is Pamela Zeilman, MSN, ANP-BC. She is a Board-Certified Nurse Practitioner, but is simply known to her colleagues as "The Wizard." Dr. Okun was also present for the exam. There were two representatives from St. Jude Medical: Randy Miller, Territory Manager – Movement Disorders, and Victor Vozzo, Regional Sales Manager – Movement Disorders. Randy had been in my second surgery where the battery was installed and would be following my case throughout all the programming sessions.

I had to be off my medications for the programming session. That was a bit disappointing because my tremor had returned by the start of my appointment at 8:00 a.m. This was necessary for Pam and Dr. Okun to view my "off med" appearance. I went through the standard Parkinson's patient exam, which included finger tapping, heel tapping, standing up and walking down the hall. These sessions would all be videotaped to allow the university to monitor the results using the new St. Jude Medical equipment.

Once the basics were handled, Pam spent about two hours testing out different settings for the device. By using the provided Apple iPod Touch, I am able to toggle between up to sixteen separate programming options. That is most likely many more choices than I will ever need. I asked if the different settings were based on activity level, such as when I was riding my bike vs. watching television. That is not the basis – it is directed more at the amount of power, which of the leads are activated, and the specific symptoms the device is attempting to control.

There is a combination of art and science in programming a DBS system. I compare it to an eye exam where you are asked, "Is one or two better?" It's rather subjective and can be a bit confusing for the patient. Over the course of the six programming sessions, both Pam and I began to feel that my setting was optimized. As such, the device was providing the maximum amount of relief for my individual set of symptoms, while not creating any unwanted side effects. Following the initial six monthly programming sessions, I will continue to meet with my programmer twice a year to monitor the system and make minor adjustments.

At its best, I would agree with others who have said that DBS surgery rolls back the level of their Parkinson's symptoms by up to five years. Previous devices provide benefits for up to ten years. An advantage of the St. Jude Medical device is that new developments with the software can easily be updated for my device without the need for additional surgeries, which could extend the usefulness of the system beyond a decade. At each session, the estimated battery life will be reviewed. The battery will have to be replaced every three to five years. That is a fairly simple, outpatient procedure.

I have turned the device off during the course of some of the presentations that I give to groups. My tremor returns immediately, which demonstrates the benefit of the device when it is on.

DBS Surgery is not a cure; however, it does provide a tremendous benefit for some patients. Having the steady flow of current to the STN region in my brain has also allowed me to reduce the amount of medication that I take by half. The balance of the DBS and the right amount of medication is the key to controlling symptoms.

I am very pleased with my DBS procedure and feel that it was the proper decision for me at this point in the progression of my Parkinson's disease. I am very grateful to my entire team at the University of Florida and St. Jude Medical for outstanding and respectful care throughout this entire process. I feel a renewed sense of confidence, knowing that the most annoying symptoms are being kept at bay for the moment. I am able to get on with living a high-quality and productive life. That is very important to me and to my family.

PD Heroes – Jill Ater – Tacoma, WA

Jill Ater with Davis at the Davis Phinney Foundation

I'm a firm believer that people enter your life just when you need them. Jill Ater would be an example of that philosophy. We were both chosen to be members of the first cohort of Davis Phinney Foundation Ambassadors in 2015. We didn't get to meet in person until the World Parkinson's Conference in September, 2016. We got to know each other through the monthly ambassador Skype calls, emails, and Facebook posts. Jill was diagnosed with Parkinson's early, at age 51.

Both Jill's mother and her sister also have PD. In our ambassador work, we have collaborated on several cases, identifying resources from various points across the country to help patients and their caregivers, including finding Spanish language support when needed through some contacts at the Mohammed Ali Parkinson's Center in Arizona.

Jill Ater has a wicked sense of humor. Sometimes one needs to draw on a bit of black humor to laugh at the insanity of their disease. Jill excels at that. She is outspoken and not shy about sharing her opinions and beliefs. We are in agreement politically and in many areas. We both believe that life is precious and people should not be denied care to simply line the pockets of insurance companies and politicians, and that the environment and the planet are important too.

When I decided to have DBS surgery, Jill immediately took me under her wing, more like a good Jewish mother than a younger friend. She had a double DBS procedure a couple of years ago. Her surgeon was Dr. Monique Giroux from Denver (who is also the author of the Davis Phinney Foundation's Every Victory Counts manual. Jill's first bit of advice was that DBS was the best thing she ever did. She answered my questions and helped put me at ease about this scary procedure. By the time I had my operation, I was very much at ease, due in part to Jill's coaching and concern for my wellbeing.

CHAPTER 19

Parkinson's Advocacy

THERE ARE A NUMBER OF WAYS to become involved in the Parkinson's Community.

- Advocating for funding for scientific research to find effective treatment options and ultimately a cure.

- Attending local Parkinson's Support Groups by attending meetings, participating in exercise classes or other activities such as Dance for PD.

- Fundraising with groups such as the Michael J. Fox Foundation's Team Fox or Davis Phinney Foundation's Victory Crew events.

- Attending seminars to increase knowledge about the latest trends in PD research and methods to improve quality of life for people living with Parkinson's and their Care Partners.

- Enrolling in clinical studies to help advance the knowledge of the disease and lead to better ways to diagnose, prevent, and treat the condition.

My skill set is mainly in the areas of organization, training and education, and connecting with people rather than advocacy at the governmental level. Over the past few years, my focus has been on helping the local Parkinson's Community, participating in clinical studies, and becoming involved regionally as a Davis Phinney Foundation Ambassador.

Parkinson Association of Central Florida

The Central Florida area is fortunate to have several support programs and services available for people living with Parkinson's and their Care Partners. The Parkinson Association of Central Florida establishes the vision and direction for programs needed by the local PD community and conducts fundraising events to bring those programs to life.

Just as Parkinson's disease is complicated and has many variations, ensuring that the needs of this diverse community are met requires a great deal of preparation and planning. Some of the information and services delivered include:

- General Parkinson-related news and updates

- Medication and drug information, news, and updates

- Educational materials, books, brochures, flyers, speakers, and events

- Local support group access (based on location and need)

The group offers a variety of programs and services to meet the needs of both the patients and caregivers. These include support group meetings, presentations, exercise classes, dance and singing classes, and connections to programs in the community to help with individual needs. They also run a Young Onset PD support group

The coordination of the programs is done by Anissa Mitchell, Parkinson Outreach Program Manager for Florida Hospital. Anissa works tirelessly to make sure that a myriad of options is available to the PD Community. Throughout the year, she makes arrangements for the following:

- Parkinson's Support Groups in multiple locations

- COPE – Care Optimally Parkinson Education for Caregivers

- PD 101 – Training for the newly diagnosed

- YOPD – Young Onset Parkinson's Support Group

- What's Shakin' Program for kids with parents or grandparents with PD

- PD Golf Program

- PWR! Parkinson Wellness Recovery Classes

- Art's the Spark – To help those with memory through art

- Movement as Medicine – Modeled after the Dance for PD Program

- Living Out Loud – LSVT Speech Program

- Cheer – Drama Therapy Classes

- Rock Steady Boxing

- Pedaling for Parkinson's Spin Classes

In addition, Anissa plans and delivers an annual symposium on behalf of Florida Hospital entitled "The Brain and Beyond Conference." The program seeks to educate, empower and equip patients, caregivers and family members with news on the latest trends in managing Parkinson's symptoms and improving quality of life. Over the past few years, Anissa has attracted some of the best minds in the Parkinson Community and most inspirational speakers, such as Dr. Michael Okun, Davis Phinney, John Baumann, and Brian Grant.

I had the privilege of serving as the Vice President of the Parkinson Association of Central Florida Board from 2013 – 2015. All of the members of the Board are volunteers and most have a direct connection to Parkinson's disease. Among them are:

- Marti Miller, President. Marti's husband, David, has Parkinson's disease. In addition to being David's primary Care Partner, she is a "force to be reckoned with" and will leave no stone unturned to ensure that the goals of the PACF are met. She's put untold hours into organizing a local Walk for Parkinson's, an annual event which brings in about $100,000 in much-needed donations.

- John Gabriel, former General Manager of the Orlando Magic, NBA Executive of the Year, and a PWP (person living with Parkinson's).

- Rita Bornstein, President Emerita Rollins College, Winter Park, FL. Also lives with Parkinson's disease while serving on multiple boards in addition to PACF.

The Parkinson Association of Central Florida and the programs offered by Florida Hospital are providing a great service to the PD Community in Central Florida.

Clinical Trials

The purpose of clinical trials is to find ways to more effectively prevent, diagnose, or treat disease. Research is taking place all around the world to better understand Parkinson's disease. Some focus on ways to properly diagnose Parkinson's disease, especially since there is no definitive way to do so at the moment. Others concentrate on ways to prevent people from contracting PD. There is a great deal of merit in that type of study, since there can be both genetic and environmental contributing factors causing the disease. Once a person has been diagnosed, there is a need to understand which medications or other treatment options are most effective at slowing, reversing, or even eradicating the disease.

For clinical trials to be meaningful, at some point human subjects must step forward and agree to take part in research studies. Clinical trials are a final and crucial step on the path to developing better treatments for Parkinson's patients today. Around the world, between 40% and 70% of trials face delays because of a lack of volunteers. One effective way to locate studies is by using the Fox Trial Finder. Here is this link: https://foxtrialfinder.michaeljfox.org/. Fox Trial Finder was created by the Michael J. Fox Foundation to help increase the flow of willing participants – both people with Parkinson's and control participants who do not have Parkinson's – into the clinical trials that need them, accelerating the Parkinson's drug development process.

In January of 2013, I learned about a study being conducted at the University of Florida by Dr. David Vaillancourt. He looked at how the brain regulates voluntary and involuntary movement with a specific focus on motor disorders. His research used advanced neuroimaging techniques to study the functional and structural changes in the brains of humans and animals that span Parkinson's disease, tremor, ataxia, and dystonia. The study being conducted at that time recruited about 80 participants, half of whom had Parkinson's disease and the other half who did not. The commitment involved in taking part in the study is two consecutive years. The goal of the study was to identify a biomarker that would assist in the diagnosis and tracking the progression of Parkinson's disease. I simply called the study the "MRI Study," however I believe that it is known as the "Parkinson's Disease Biomarker Program," or PDBP, which is a federally funded research program.

The study took place over one full day. I did it the first time in January, 2014. It involved a blood draw, which should have been labeled as the "Vampire blood draw," since at least 12-15 vials of blood were taken. The second part was done in an MRI machine. I should clearly state that I've never been a big fan of MRIs. In the past, even for a short MRI, I would always opt for some form of sedation due to a feeling of claustrophobia in the tight space. For this study, I was not allowed to take anything to calm my nerves and I was required to be off my Parkinson's medication (Carbidopa-Levodopa). I was directed to the MRI room and the technician had me lie down on the table. Then she put a clear mask over my face that was touching my nose. I told her that wouldn't work, so she removed some padding, which gave me a tiny bit of clearance space.

The technician didn't mess around. Once she determined that I was all set, she popped me into the tube. The difference with this MRI was that I was able to view a computer monitor above my head. Prior to going into the tube, I was trained for about 45 minutes on a computer game that involved depressing a button on a device and matching lines up on the computer monitor. I had been given the controller with the button prior to going into the tube, and soon the computer game commenced. I played that for about a half-hour, which did provide some distraction. After the game was finished, they asked me to tell them what type of music I preferred to listen to and they put on some jazz. That didn't matter because all I could hear was the banging and clanging of the machine. The total time in the MRI was an hour and a half. Surprisingly, I didn't kick down the walls or start screaming or crying. I figured that I'd "taken one for the team" by doing my bit in the MRI that day.

Next, there were several cognitive tests. Quizzes like repeating long strings of random numbers and letters, which makes you doubt your sanity. That was followed by manual dexterity activities, manipulating objects, which was a challenge due to my rigidity. If this was child's play, I felt that I wouldn't make a very good kid anymore. The last portion of the day was spent in a gym doing several physical activities to test my balance, flexibility and agility. I was pleased to hear the technician tell me that my balance was very good. I attributed some of that to my bicycle riding. In January, 2015, I went through the entire process once again. This time I at least knew what to expect.

The problem with most studies of this nature is that you never find out the results. I have learned that this particular study has identified some biomarkers that the researchers are able to follow to determine changes in cognitive function and motor function changes. This discovery led Dr. Vaillancourt to the conclusion that suggests that resistance training (basically lifting weights) could be a way to control the progression of the disease. It's exciting to see that this clinical research may be pointing to some ways to help people with Parkinson's.

There are a variety of clinical studies being conducted at any time. Candidates are reviewed to make sure that they are a proper fit for a specific study. A participant always has the right to stop taking part in a study at any time. Research takes a long time to conduct, but it depends greatly on people enrolling in clinical trials to advance the learning that can be of benefit in the long run.

Brain Donation

I recently enrolled in a program called the National DBS Brain Tissue Network as a Brain Tissue Donor. There is a great shortage of brain tissue for the study of many neurodegenerative disorders, including Parkinson's disease. My donation will provide researchers with an opportunity to better understand these disorders and provide insight on improving treatments and medications.

No one wants to think about their own mortality. However, many people are very willing to sign organ donor cards to donate other vital organs to help extend another person's life or to use for research. If I can help someone in the future by donating my brain, I am glad to do so. However, I will hopefully keep using it myself for a very long time.

I feel a very close alliance with the University of Florida. When we moved to Florida in 1989, I didn't know much about or have any ties to any of the universities in the state. I graduated from Michigan State University (The School of Hospitality Business). My son graduated from the University of Southern California Film School. However, I entrusted my daughter's education to the University of Florida. Therefore, my money went there too. As you saw in the previous chapter, I chose UF for my DBS surgery and now have plans to donate my brain to this fine institution. I must say that I'm fairly tightly connected with this Gainesville campus now – and forever. Go Gators!

Davis Phinney Foundation Ambassador Program

In 2014, the Davis Phinney Foundation for Parkinson's created an Ambassador Program. I was honored to be selected as one of the initial cohort of ten to serve in this capacity. The role of the Ambassadors is to share the Foundation's resources and information throughout their local and regional communities and to help people with Parkinson's take action and improve their quality of life.

The Ambassador Program was led by Ally Ley, Davis Phinney Foundation Program Specialist, and Heather Caldwell, Davis Phinney Foundation Program Manager. I had met Ally at the Ride With Larry, since that was her first assignment for the foundation. I have always respected her enthusiasm and joyful spirit. Ally did a fantastic job in organizing, training, and motivating this group – which was spread around the country – by conducting monthly conference calls and keeping in touch with each of us personally.

I consider each of the other Ambassadors to be PD Heroes in their own right. Many are accomplished cyclists, having participated in events such as Ride the Rockies, RAGBRAI, Copper Triangle, POPS Ride, or solo rides across the country. They each embody the philosophy of "Living Well Today" with Parkinson's. The common thread that runs through the group is the desire to make others aware of the fact that there are options available that help people with Parkinson's to have a better quality of life.

We were each given the freedom to schedule our time based on our personal availability. It was interesting to see the various ways that the Ambassadors chose to share their knowledge. Everyone set about manning Davis Phinney Foundation information tables at local and regional workshops, Parkinson's Walks, and other events. Whenever possible, presentations were delivered to share both the Davis Phinney Foundation message as well as our personal PD journeys. While sharing information with large and small groups was rewarding, we all found one-on-one meetings with individuals to be particularly meaningful. It was enriching to provide a newly diagnosed person with practical tools to cope with this major change in their life – and to let them know that there was hope.

197

The first meeting that I attended as an Ambassador was a Young Onset Parkinson's Support Group session in Orlando. There were about ten people present and I shared the basics about the Foundation and handed out cards for the participants to order complimentary copies of the "Every Victory Counts" manuals. A representative from Compass Research also told the group about his organization's programs and brought pizza for the group. I only had one slice of pizza, but was experiencing back pains throughout the balance of the meeting. A half-hour after going to bed, I woke up with piercing pain in my chest as well as my back. Thinking that this was a heart attack, we called an ambulance and I was taken to the emergency room. Turns out that I was having a gall bladder attack. After getting over that, I met with a surgeon and scheduled a gall bladder removal procedure. I didn't realize that the gall bladder was a "throw away" organ. I've done very well ever since without it.

World Parkinson's Congress

In September, 2016, all the Ambassadors were invited to represent the Davis Phinney Foundation at the World Parkinson's Congress in Portland, OR. This event is held every three years. There were 4,550 attendees from 67 countries around the globe. The participants included medical professionals (neurologists, neurosurgeons, physical therapists, occupational therapists, dieticians, researchers, etc.). 2,284 of the participants were either people with Parkinson's, Care Partners, or family members. It was an incredibly energizing several days, which included large and small group presentations as well as opportunities to interact with the best minds who were focused on understanding and treating this condition. I've gone to many conferences and conventions throughout my working career, but none as enriching as this one. I could have gone to completely different sessions two times over and still not seen everything. I left with a renewed feeling of hope and optimism knowing that so many people were jointly focused on improving the lives of people with Parkinson's.

Helping out in the Davis Phinney Foundation booth was a highlight of the week. So many people came up and shared their stories about how this group's work had made an impact on their lives. I particularly enjoyed introducing the Foundation's programs to people who were not familiar with them and were seeking exactly this type of quality resource. I met a young man who had recently been diagnosed with Young Onset Parkinson's disease. He and his wife had done a great deal of research but had reached "information overload." I was able to confirm some of the things that they had discovered and guide them in other directions about others. Even though they lived in Tennessee, they had decided to come down to the University of Florida for a consultation. As it turns out, my entire medical team from UF was at the conference, so I could introduce them prior to his scheduled appointment. I also invited them to join us for dinner, which gave them a chance to meet some other YOPD patients. Creating those connections made the trip worthwhile for me.

The next World Parkinson's Congress is scheduled for Kyoto, Japan in 2019. I can at least dream about attending that one. If I am able to attend, I could display my book in their "Book Nook" section. Perhaps if I sell enough copies of "The Journey Begins With 1,000 Miles," I'll be able to go. (Thank you for buying a copy – please tell your friends to purchase one as well!)

PD Heroes – Bob Harmon – Lake Wales, FL

" I tee it up for Team Fox every day because being an active part of this community is better than a hole in one! "

Bob Harmon
Golf for the Cure
Team Fox member living with PD

Bob Harmon was diagnosed with Parkinson's disease in 2006, while he was in his early 50s. He strongly believes in the therapeutic value of exercise, so he has continued to play golf, taken up Tai Chi, and even completed a prestigious 10K race at Walt Disney World.

When he realized that there were no support services in his rural Florida community, Bob founded a PD support group that now regularly attracts 70 attendees to each session. Bob spends hours of his own time researching the latest PD news and information to share with the group.

Bob has taken part in numerous clinical trials to advance research. One such trial involved spending time each day on his computer to improve his cognitive memory skills.

Bob is very involved with the Michael J. Fox Foundation. They regularly ask him to serve as a panelist at their Partners in Parkinson's events, usually helping to demonstrate how to effectively meet with a Movement Disorder Specialist to educate the audience on this important encounter.

Bob is also a Team Fox VIP. He founded a *Golf for the Cure* event in Lake Ashton, Florida. This annual tournament has raised over $350,000 for the Michael J. Fox Foundation. Not only is Bob an overall good guy, he is a role model for others living with PD.

CHAPTER 20

Looking Forward

I VIEW PARKINSON'S AS BOTH A BLESSING AND A CALLING. It is a blessing because it has allowed me to meet the most amazing and inspirational people, which in turn has helped me to accept and deal with this condition in a positive, optimistic way. From the time that I was in college, I have been considered a natural connector. I have a knack for bringing people together and pairing up those in need with resources. That is a key reason why my role as a Davis Phinney Foundation Ambassador is a perfect fit. It allows me to provide the Parkinson's community with resources to lighten their burdens and bring them joy. I believe that the Davis Phinney Foundation's philosophy gives people hope and skills to cope with Parkinson's disease like no other group. They embrace five basic tenets, which offer wise advice for coping with Parkinson's.

Be Informed

- Gather information from reliable sources.

- Find the facts you need, but don't get overwhelmed.

- Attend a Davis Phinney Foundation Victory Summit, Michael J. Fox Partners in Parkinson event, or a workshop sponsored by your local PD Association or Major Hospital.

Be Connected

- Take advantage of local support groups.

- Young Onset patients, find a YOPD group in your area. If one doesn't exist, start one.

- Look for inspiration within and outside the PD Community.

Be Active

- Exercise regularly. Anything is better than nothing. Consider walking, swimming, cycling, dancing, yoga, tai chi, or any activity that you enjoy.

- Track your exercise. Compete against yourself.

- Consider taking a PWR! class or enroll in a Rock Steady Boxing program.

Be Engaged

- Take control of your Parkinson's by being proactive in your treatment plan. Be your own best advocate.

- Build your own PD team to address all your needs.

- Support your local PD community, offer your talents.

- Be courageous.

- We can't control that we have Parkinson's, but we can control how we choose to live with it.

- Be mindful of your daily Moments of Victory and be sure to celebrate them.

- Choose to be a role model or inspiration to someone else.

Thriving Despite Parkinson's

Michael J. Fox once said, "I have no choice about whether I have Parkinson's. I have nothing but choices about how I react to it. In those choices, there's freedom to do a lot of things in areas that I wouldn't have otherwise found myself in."

As I see it, a person can go one of three routes after receiving news of a diagnosis such as Parkinson's disease. They can bury their head in the sand and become a recluse and let whatever is going to happen control their lives. They can choose to "survive," meaning taking their medication and not doing much else. The third choice is to thrive. The definition of "thrive" is to grow vigorously, to make steady progress, to prosper, and to flourish. How can one thrive with a degenerative disease? Following the five basic tenets described above is one way. But it's not the only way; find something that works for you. While Parkinson's does take things away from people, it also offers the opportunity to grow, change, and connect in new ways.

The following acronym for "THRIVING" may be a useful way to look at the challenge called Parkinson's disease – to analyze your status in the progression and take control of your own personal outcome. I created the acronym as a way to not only deal with a disease like Parkinson's but with any personal challenge. That could be a business, career, or relationship issue that you need to address. This approach has served me well in dealing with the unexpected introduction of Parkinson's in my life and how I have chosen to handle it. The THRIVING approach applies equally well in other circumstances.

T – Turmoil. The initial diagnosis is unsettling. Take time to process it, even grieve a bit if you need to. Your life will be changing. However, like many changes that you have made over time, there is still room for good things to happen.

H – Honest Assessment. Get the facts. Parkinson's is not a death sentence. Most likely, no matter what age it begins, it will be with you for a long time. What is the state of your overall health?

R – Research. Learn what you need to know to deal with this condition in the best way possible. Don't get overwhelmed by information. Absorb more knowledge over time.

I – Initiative. Become your own advocate for your care. Build a support team, which should include your family, friends, a PD support network, informed medical specialists such as movement disorder specialists, physical therapists, occupational therapists, speech therapists, etc.

V – Victory. Set goals and strive to achieve them. Any physical activity is better than nothing. Try new things – walking, swimming, riding a bike, boxing, yoga. Keep your brain active and alert – it's another muscle, after all. Take up painting, singing, or a musical instrument. Celebrate your victories, small or large.

I – Inspiration. Seek out people who inspire you – the choice is yours. Build your own list of PD Heroes and communicate with them. Share what you know with others; you may just be the inspiration they need. To the world, you may just be one person – but to one person, you may be the world.

N – Never Give Up. Winston Churchill said, "Never yield to the apparently overwhelming might of the enemy." PD is your enemy – you must push back against it.

G – Gratitude. Sure, you've been dealt a bad hand. But there is still so very much to be grateful for every day. Take time to count your blessings and share your gratitude with those who have had meaning in your life.

Having a plan and choosing to thrive will arm you against some of the challenges that you will face in living with Parkinson's. Be patient with yourself and leave room for adjustments along the way. If you find yourself slipping from time to time, remember the words of the old song, "Pick yourself up, dust yourself off, and start all over again." Doing your best is all that you can expect of yourself. However, by making the attempt, you are capable of creating your own hope for the future. It's your life – Parkinson's is only a visitor that is along for the ride.

I've created a motto which keeps me focused on living well with having Parkinson's. It is a reminder that everything will be all right, that we should be constantly grateful. And that we should continue to move forward one pedal stroke at a time. I hope you find it useful in your own journey forward.

Gratitude

There are so many people to whom I owe a debt of gratitude. Taking on the adventures I have done since my PD diagnosis would not have been possible without their support.

Cycling Savvy

Cycling Savvy is by far the best bike skills training program in the country – I have used every one of the lessons that I learned in that course during my various bike rides and truly felt "empowered for unlimited travel."

Cycling Savvy Program Founders: Thank you for following through on your vision of turning bike riders into bike drivers. I sincerely appreciate the time and patience that you showed to me not only in class, but for the after course follow-up and invitations to group rides.

- Keri Caffrey
- Mighk Wilson

Cycling Savvy Instructors: I'm sure that I'm overlooking a number of CSIs (Cycling Savvy Instructors), but these are the ones that come to mind. All CSIs go through extensive training in order to qualify to teach this important class.

- Lisa Walker
- Heidi Leavey
- Rodney Youngblood
- Jason Buckner
- Kitzzy Avilles
- Keith McLane

- Pamela Murray
- Karen and Howard Karabell
- John Brookings
- William Carpenter
- Richard Wharton
- John S. Allen
- John Schubert

Riding Friends

- Larry Gies - (Rode with me on Ride 4 Ronald Metric Century)
- Kathy Leblanc-Bliss (Rode with me on Ride 4 Ronald Metric Century)
- Stix Cook
- Doug and June Murray
- Brad and Darlyn Kuhn
- Edwina McGee (A.F.)
- John McMahon (met on a Viking River Cruise in the Netherlands. John brought his bike with him on a family trip to Florida in order to ride with me.)

Bike Shop Owners

- Michael and Arden Cottle - Out-Spoke'n Bike Shop - Lake Mary, FL. My "go-to" bike shop. I bought my Electra Townie from these great folks. Always helpful in keeping me rolling over the years by providing great service.

- Jessica and Dana Kinney - Retro City Cycles - Orlando, FL. Terrific supporters of the Orlando cycling community.

University of Florida Center for Movement Disorder and Neurorestoration Medical Team

The following members of the UF team, along with the rest of their staff, has provided outstanding care to me ever since I began going there in 2013. I have no reservations in recommending the UF Team to anyone seeking top-notch care and monitoring of Parkinson's. They are caring, knowledgeable, and professional in every aspect of their service. They sincerely place the needs of the patient first.

- Dr. Michael Okun - Neurologist
- Dr. Kelly Foote - Neurosurgeon
- Dr. Irene Malaty - Neurologist
- Pam Zeilman - DBS programming Wizard
- Lisa Warren - Occupational Therapist
- Meredith DiFranco - Physical Therapist
- Frances Rivera - Social Worker

Abbott/St. Jude Medical

- Randy Miller - Territory Rep. Randy has been my "wing man" from the point of my DBS Surgeries and throughout every one of my DBS programming sessions. I have been able to call him and get a prompt response every time. He genuinely listens and cares about my needs and concerns. The DBS process went smoothly in large part to Randy's genuine concern, his professional knowledge and outstanding follow through.

- I'm also grateful to the St. Jude Medical Neurostimulation Division Sales leader, Brian Faldetta, for inviting me to present to their sales team at their national meeting in Orlando in February 2017. Also, for placing an advance order for a copies of my book for all of his team.

Family

While both of my parents had passed away before my diagnosis with Parkinson's, I owe a great deal of the way that I have coped with this condition to the approach that they taught me when I was young and the joyful and positive outlook that they each had about life in general. I have always tried to emulate their positive attitudes in everything that I do.

I am grateful to have been able to pick up the phone at any time and call my brother, Chuck, or sister, Cindy, as I have been learning to deal with my Parkinson's diagnosis. They are both great listeners and care a tremendous amount for my wellbeing and for my own family.

I dedicated this book to my wife, Laura, but want to also thank her for her patience with me since PD entered our lives. She has been patient with the time that my bike riding and other exercise have taken away from family time. She's also accepted that I'm a bit slower and more fatigued at times. I appreciate her understanding.

I am very appreciative of the ways in which my son, Brian, and my daughter, Jennifer, have supported and encouraged me.

They have joined me on bike rides, participated with me in triathlons, and cheered me on every step of the way. I couldn't have asked for two better kids. I also thank their spouses (Brian's Jessica and Jen's Bob) for sharing them with me to do these activities and for their own support.

Support Team

Roger Barr - My best friend in the whole wide world. Thank you, Roger, for taking me to the top of the mountain and for always being there for a wee chat. Wish I could see you in person on a more regular basis, but I always know that you are there for me.

Ability Rehab - Lake Mary, FL. This is my local physical therapy facility, which helped me when I was recovering from my torn rotator cuff and total shoulder replacement. They were always kind, but pushed me to regain maximum mobility.

- David

- Kelly

- Sondra

Parkinson Association of Central Florida - It was an honor to serve on the board of this fine organization for two years. While there have been, and currently are, many other members of the board, I had the most involvement with the following individuals.

- Marti Miller

- John Gabriel

- Rita Bornstein

- Gail Fisher

Davis Phinney Foundation - I was so very fortunate to find this group early on. The information that they provide to the PD Community is invaluable. I have learned a great deal from them, and had the privilege of representing them as an Ambassador for the past two years. I am so grateful for their kindness, love, and ongoing support.

- Davis Phinney
- Connie Carpenter Phinney
- Polly Dawkins
- Ally Ley
- Heather Caldwell
- Chris Brewer
- Lauren Kehn

Contributors

I am very grateful to all of the friends and family who have responded to my requests for donations for the various rides that I took part in to increase Parkinson's awareness.

Book Editing and Publishing

While I did the writing, it takes a great team to see a book through to actually being published and available to the public. From encouragement in the beginning, to helpful reviews and critiques to improve the content, to working with a very talented and supportive book coach, I was on a clear path to success with the following people in my corner.

Monique Donahue - Monique initially offered to help me self-publish my book and provided some initial guidance and direction. I took quite a while to get started on the book, but she at least helped me understand and believe that I could actually do it.

I appreciate the time that my son, Brian Alexander, spent on reviewing the first draft of this book. His skills as a television writer were very helpful in terms of bringing clarity to my writing. I say that any writing ability that I have was due to reverse genetics from my son. The fact that Brian actually participated with me on the Ride With Larry also gave him great insight into my story and helped him to provide me with very useful comments. He was a kind but tough critic, causing me to improve many parts of the book.

I am incredibly grateful to my book coach, Amy Collette. Teaming up with Amy reassured me that I could actually follow through and complete the book in a reasonable period of time. We started with a book planning session and together created a master plan. Once I had completed the first draft, I sent it to Amy for editing. She also did the layout for the book and directed me to a member of her team for the book cover design. The fact that Amy is closely connected to the Davis Phinney Foundation through the Friends for Phinney made our working relationship all that much more meaningful. I felt like I was working with a member of the family, most certainly with a very trusted friend. Amy, I would not have gotten the book done in such a timely manner without you. Thank you! Check out Amy's book, *The Gratitude Connection* (available on Amazon.com)

Melody Christian was my book cover designer. I have received so many compliments from everyone that I have shown the cover to leading up to publication. Her artistic sense will make the book stand out wherever it is on display. I appreciate her talent and how easy it was to work with her.

Melissa Lyttle shot the cover photo image. She did this as part of The Parkinson's Project. She was a treat to work with and her photos were fantastic.

Promotion

I am very grateful to Daisey Charlotte, the videographer who put together my speaker's video reel to help me share my message with individuals who may consider me as an inspirational speaker for their event. Daisey did a great job of capturing the best moments from several interviews and videos of my past presentations. It turned out very well in my opinion.

Thank you to Jacie Ames, daughter of my PD buddy Carl Ames. Jacie runs Ames Graphics and has a great sense of what it takes to spotlight a person's branding image and messaging in a fantastic website. Check out her work at johnalexandertalks.com

Jerry Fabyanic, Host of the Writer's Corner, Clear Creek, Colorado, was kind enough to interview me on his radio program on May 6, 2017. It was a pleasure to share the key points from the book and my overall message with Jerry. Also, it was an honor to be recognized professionally by him as a fellow author.

Abbot Laboratories, as part of their PR for the Infinity DBS System, has made arrangements for me to take part in several radio interviews, television interviews, photo shoots, and video shoots. In particular, it has been a pleasure to appear on:

- American Medicine Today: Hosts Ethan Yount and Kimberly Bernel did a radio interview earlier in the year, which turned into a brief television piece as well. We followed that up with a television interview for their show for Bloomberg Television, which will air during the late summer of 2017. That includes interviews with my DBS doctors, Dr. Kelly Foote and Dr. Michael Okun. I appreciated Ethan and Kimberly's kindness and patience with me during the taping of these segments.

To all the many other friends and family who have supported me on my journey - thank you so very much. One never walks, or pedals, alone!

About the Author

My parents instilled in me a strong sense of faith. That included a belief that God is good and that he will provide, balanced with an understanding the God helps those who help themselves.

I've always believed in utilizing my strengths. My strengths include: a love of learning, a pursuit of excellence, a very positive and enthusiastic attitude, a desire to achieve, and a compulsion to win others over, and the ability to connect people with others and resources that I feel will benefit them. After my diagnosis, I drew upon all of those strengths to not only cope, but to thrive with Parkinson's.

This book, naturally, should appeal to all people with Parkinson's and those who care for them – their medical team and their caregivers. I particularly hope that newly diagnosed and Young Onset patients will take the time to read it and glean some of the lessons that apply to their situations.

I also wrote the book for people, in general, who are dealing with health, life or work issues. By following the "THRIVE" process, just about any challenge can become manageable.

Made in the USA
Columbia, SC
01 August 2017